Calm Down
Lift Up

Into Joy, Peace and Creativity

Calm Down
Lift Up

Into Joy, Peace and Creativity

LESLIE SANN

ALSO BY LESLIE SANN

LIFE HAPPENS:
What Are YOU Going to Do About It?

"In her new book *Calm Down Lift Up* Leslie Sann performs a miracle. She communicates the wisdom of the ages in easily readable chapters, in a language that anyone can understand and she anchors each pearl of wisdom in experiences that are familiar to all of us. In doing so she provides us with countless tools to travel the road of life with increased happiness, creativity and fulfillment. I will definitely recommend this book to all my clients and students. Thank you, Leslie, this book is truly masterful."

Dr. Bertrand Babinet
Author of *Empowering the Heart*
www.babinetics.com

༄༃

"Leslie Sann has written a spiritually beguiling book that invites the reader to experience the power of love, freedom and creativity to be found in the stillness and silence waiting to embrace us when the mind calms down … a perfect antidote for our age of anxiety."

Steve Chandler
Author of *Time Warrior*
www.stevechandler.com

༄༃

"I love this book. What a treasure. I am totally convinced that anyone reading Leslie's book who practices even one of the many easy to learn skills and perspectives will experience a life change for the better. Plus, she makes it easy to understand, practice, and know when you've made a positive shift."

H. Ronald Hulnick, Ph.D.,
Co-author of *Loyalty to Your Soul: The Heart of Spiritual Psychology*
www.universityofsantamonica.edu

Calm Down Lift Up
Into Joy, Peace and Creativity

Living by Design Press
leslie@living-bydesign.com

ISBN-13:
978-1-7353677-0-5

Cover Art & Photograph Copyright ©2020
by Daniel deMoulin/Nourish Media Inc.
www.nourishcreative.com

This book is dedicated to John-Roger

Thank you J-R

Table of Contents

Preface

I'm sitting in my rocker that I've positioned to face the back of my property. It is a still, cold, January morning with a partly cloud-covered winter sky. I see the old farmhouse where Jerry and Ann live. The house is up on the hill beyond the fence row that divides our parcels. The space between our homes is covered with snow.

My attention is on the birds at the feeder. Make that feeders. I see finches, titmice, chickadees, juncos, woodpeckers. I love it when the gang of mourning doves nestles together underneath the covered feeder filled with food, cooing their appreciation for the shelter.

It seems, temporarily, that the raccoon bandit who has been raiding my feeders has found another place to feast. I had been away and there was no food out and she must have found other territory. That doesn't mean she won't be back, but now I have Trapper Steve on my side. If she does return, he will humanely remove her to another place in the world to live. I don't want her moving into my attic to have babies in the spring.

Meeting life on life's terms.

Today I'll add to the wood pile in the garage as it's going to get very cold and I'd rather do that in 20° weather than -10° below.

As I'm sitting here gently rocking, watching the bird activity, I am also watching my thoughts. I'm aware there is a disturbance of energy moving through my mind. I track it backwards and find it was triggered by something I read on the Internet having to do with world affairs.

That thought leads me to another, which is a repetition of something I read. The article stated that 80% of the population surveyed reported having anxiety. Another thought chimes in that the statistic was not surprising considering how much negative news is broadcast.

Yet here I sit watching snow-covered beauty, calm and undisturbed. I see a red cardinal land on the roof of the feeder. I follow its movements as it drops to the ground and begins poking around for seed.

I reflect on how many anxiety attacks I have lived through in my life. They rose up and took me into crazy-land, panicked, convinced that this time the sky was surely going to fall. Like a storm on the sea, giant waves of fearful thoughts came pounding in my head, threatening to capsize the boat of my well-being.

Have you ever played with a pinwheel? It is a toy consisting of curls of paper or plastic loosely attached by a pin to a stick. When you blow on it, or when it is blown by the wind, it revolves around the center pin. If you look at it closely while it is in motion you will notice at the very center there is no movement. Everything is moving around the center still-point.

Over the years I've learned to quiet myself down to my center-still-point while lifting up to my place of peace and joy and creativity. My life is now more like a boat rocking gently on the ocean near the shore. There are still ups and downs, of course; life still has weather, and I seem to have developed a greater capacity to find my center while the waters of life are rocking the boat.

Watching the birds enjoying their breakfast, watching the clouds make way for blue sky and sun, watching my thoughts float through, I am aware of the presence of stillness.

Gazing out the window, enjoying the clouds moving away as the sun turns the snow an even brighter white, I hear another voice among my thoughts: I am still here.

I am reminded of a conversation I had with a client years ago. She had arrived in a great deal of distress and eventually, through the process of our session, landed in a quiet, calm, peaceful place of deep tranquility. Speaking from this serene place, she declared, I am still here.

Inviting her to be curious, I asked her to explore the phrase. I invite you to join me right now.

I am still here.

No matter how long you've walked on this planet, breathed the oxygen available to you, put yourself to bed, gotten yourself up and out in the morning — no matter how much negative news has been reported, or even how much negative news has been experienced directly in your life — you are still here.

We get through it. One day the body won't make it. Until that moment we are still here.

I suggested to my client she emphasize the I AM in the phrase.

I AM still here.

Hmmm …

In some traditions I AM is a representation of the Divine, the Magnificent Mystery, I AM.

I AM still here.

Perhaps the divine is always with us. Perhaps who we really are is divine.

I then encouraged her to shift the emphasis to the word STILL.

I am STILL here.

When we drop into the quiet, unmoving center there is stillness. Can you find it right now? Put the book down and turn your attention inward. Take a breath and relax. Let yourself discover the stillness within.

Hmmm ...

I then encouraged her to shift the emphasis to the word HERE.

I am still HERE.

This place of quiet tranquility, of calm, of stillness, is found in the present moment. HERE. Now. Always right here.

Shift your attention and find if this might be true for you.

Perhaps you could take these four words into your morning contemplation, if you have one. If not, you could take a walk and examine the phrase: I am still here. Allow the phrase to reveal its gifts.

No matter what has gone on in your life, or is going on in your life right now, or you imagine might be going on in your life in the next moment, or week or year from now, you are still here.

When you bring yourself to the stillness of here and of now, you will find a place of calm — the peace that surpasses understanding.

Always with you.

Always here.

Now.

Introduction

In my more than 30 years of serving people as an educator, mentor, counselor and coach, sharing an abundance of practical spiritual tools, I have discovered that learning to calm down is the most powerful life skill a person can develop.

If you are wound like a top, whirling and driven, there is no space for creativity, wonder or joy. If you are spinning, spinning, spinning, moved by outside forces, there is no quiet to hear your inner wisdom guide you. You live as a victim to stress. Life is, quite frankly, miserable.

There is no urgency when we are calm. When we Calm Down and Lift Up, we have access to the well of our being, which is filled with tools and capacities to move us forward in the moment. There is space and, in that space we can hear wisdom speak.

We calm down so we can lift up.

Conscious **A**wareness **L**ifting **M**e up

What does that mean? When we are calm, present to this very moment, we are our most creative, resourceful selves. We lift up out of survival-brain reactivity into the higher human-brain creativity. (Note: the words *reactivity* and *creativity* have the same letters!)

When we lift up, we move into the space of inventiveness, resourcefulness, humor, spiritual intelligence, innovation and more. From Up here we can figure out anything. This place of calm, and the willingness to embrace circumstances, is where we find our resilient spirit. Our resilience recognizes *life happening* as an opportunity to engage creativity and step into the possibility of finding solutions to our problems, designing a future we prefer to live in. Powerful.

Power is defined as the ability to take action. Creative action. Effective action. Useful action.

When we calm down, we come present to our power. Our ability to do, to create, to change, to grow into something *next*. Something even better. This *Calm Down Lift Up* book is designed to serve you in doing so, over and over and over again. Why so many overs? Because life is designed to upset us. It disturbs us on purpose in order to wake us up to even more goodness in our lives. Prodding us out of bed, to go to school to learn and grow, and evolve into the next best version of ourselves.

Life is a classroom. The curriculum of life is that of gaining experience for learning and growing. Those who love to learn thrive amidst the circumstances they find themselves. They know the goal is not to change the school. The goal is to graduate.

What does graduate look like? Lifting up into the recognition of who you truly are.

Now, you don't have to do this. Lots of folks don't. Many live in 'upset' most of the time and have loads of good reasons for doing so. That's okay. Everyone has been given the same gift: the freedom to choose. And, we each get to live in the consequences of our choices. Choose what works for you.

When I'm upset, I miss out on a lot of goodness in life. Years ago, I remember observing myself in the midst of an internal stink storm while hiking in beautiful country. The day was lovely, yet I wasn't having any of it. I was so internally upset that I could have been in a dungeon or solitary confinement. Something had happened and I was upset, ruining my life in my head. The contrast between the beauty of the nature walk and the ugly of my mind was profound. I was a prisoner to my thinking. At that time, I just didn't know what to do about it. It was like quicksand, sucking me into even more darkness and despair.

Maybe you have had a moment (or even two) like that. It is hell. I call it running around the Hamster Wheel of Hades, and there is no way off the wheel unless you know how to shift up into a higher consciousness — a place where there are no rules, no judgments, no shoulds or should nots, no right or wrong thinking. A place where life just is what it is, and we are engaging with it as it is.

Easy.

Well, the truth is, it *is* easy because it is our natural state. We just covered up the ease of joyful living with a lot of thinking and stories and expectations and what not.

The journey back to our joyous spirit is in remembering to forget anything and everything that isn't contributing to the blessing of this moment. *Here and now.* This moment as it is. Inhaling and exhaling this glorious gift of Life.

Regardless of our circumstances.

If you've ever had your version of ruining your life in your head, you have come to the right place. Time to clear your mind. This book will be like getting a power wash on the inside, cleaning away the stinking thinking that is producing misery and despair; replacing it with a fresh new look. A look that will shine from the inside out.

I'm guessing you don't want to drive through your life missing the whole thing because you were upset throughout the entire journey. You don't want to arrive at the end of your life and discover you don't remember how you got there.

So, let's do something different. Joy is present *here and now*. My aim is to help you let go of stress, move into calm, access your power to create a life you love, one moment at a time. Let's go for a joyride as you learn to Calm Down and Lift Up.

You Already Know This

*Wisdom is all within you, knowledge is all within you,
strength is all within you. There is nothing you can get
from outside. Simply, it has to be triggered. Choose
a science that can trigger the best in you.*

Yogi Bhajani

༄༅

I was in a seminar years ago and the facilitator explained the definition of educate. She shared that the word comes from the Latin, 1*educare, meaning to call forward from within. She was explaining that though she was in 'front of the room' in the position of teacher, the reality was that she was merely triggering what we already knew.

It was a shift in perspective for me. When I was a child there were the authorities and then there was me. I

learned from them. They taught me. They knew what I did not.

---

1 * *Etymologically, the word education is derived from edu-care (Latin) "bring up", which is related to educere "bring out, bring forth what is within, bring out potential" and ducere, "to lead."*

To discover the true meaning of the process of education, which is to remind me of what I already know, was empowering. It allowed me to shift focus from the outer teacher, the one appearing before me with my physical eyes, to the inner teacher, the one that I am coming to recognize as my true source of wisdom and knowing.

As you read this book remember: all wisdom lies within. Use the words written here to awaken you to what you already know. I am here to remind you of your resourcefulness, resilience, loving essence and creative intelligence. Creative intelligence is where intelligence meets imagination and is turned into useful action.

Learning to Calm Down and Lift Up is a process of remembering ourselves back to the source of peace, the power to overcome adversity, the Magnificent Mystery that dwells within. Living life to the fullest is a process of learning and discovery leading to an awakening to, or remembering of, who we truly are.

Making Good Use of this Book

We get pulled into this world through our mind, emotions and our body — moved around by circumstances — living in the chaos of life happening — running around going nowhere. We forget everything is moving around the center still-point, that there is a place to come Home to. Consider this a guidebook on your journey in remembering that Home is always present.

This book started out as part of an online learning program. What you have in your hand was a guidebook for the ten audio lessons and several video lessons, four meditations, plus bonus materials, all designed to support learning to Calm Down and Lift Up. (Access can be found at my website.)

People who took the course found it helpful. Many said they used the meditations on a daily basis. Several asked me to tell them more. This book was written to fulfill that request. That kernel of the guidebook has popped itself into this book.

As I mentioned in my previous book, *Life Happens: What Are YOU Going to Do About It?*, reading about life isn't the same as living it. You can watch YouTube videos, TED talks, read books and go to workshops, yet nothing will change, other than perhaps the height of the pile of books on your nightstand, each one holding a promise. The promise of a morsel of wisdom from Out-There that will change your life In-Here.

Change happens when we *participate*. The *willingness* to experiment through action is the difference that will make a difference. This is how we learn and grow.

The tools and practices I'm about to share are simple and life changing—if you use them. Experiment with my suggestions. Discover what works *for you*. Doing is key. Action changes lives. Don't take my word for it. Check it out. You empower yourself with your *choices* and *actions*.

This book contains stories, reflections, exercises, insights. Use it as a resource. You may read the book in the order I have laid out. You can also look at the table of contents, choose a chapter and begin. Perhaps there is value in finding the chapter which is most applicable to where you are right now. Or you might open the book randomly and see what is there.

Some of the chapters have a suggestion of something to do. I've entitled those sections, 'RX: Do This —' After all, this book is meant to be useful. You may even decide to write in the book

And now, we begin.

1. You Are More Than You Think You Are

Waking up to who you are requires letting go of whom you imagine yourself to be.

Alan Watts

༄༅

Years ago, when I was in my 20s, I participated in a 7-day Vipassana retreat. For those of you who are unfamiliar, it's a period of time of sitting meditation in silence. We would break up the sitting meditation with silent walking meditation. Meals were silent. No talking on breaks.

What we were doing was withdrawing our attention from what is called the outer word, Out-There, in order to discover something deeper than the mind, the emotions and our habitual response to life, In-Here. We were setting ourselves up to experience what is deeper than who we thought ourselves to be.

I'm sure it was the first time I spent seven days without speaking. I thoroughly enjoyed it. I love quiet, which is why I now live in the country. In this process I discovered the quiet calm that lives within each of us, a space beyond the chatter of the mind and the yo-yo of emotions.

We were instructed to watch our breath ...

In–Out–In–Out

When we discovered we were no longer watching the breath, but instead were engaged in thinking or feeling, we were to track back to the moment when we lost our attention. We were learning to observe, to notice, to be the witness of our experience.

At first, I noticed what triggered my distraction, my loss of presence, was something physical. Perhaps I would hear a bird chirp and my mind, which is designed to make meaning out of everything, would pull out a file from the memory system. It would show me an image of a bird. Then I might see a walk through a woods that I had traveled in the past where I had heard birdsong. Another folder would open, as in more think-ing, which would lead to a different thought. I was no longer present to observing the In–Out of my breath. I was lost in my mind's imaging.

I was fascinated to discover the maze of thinking the mind can create. Thinking triggered thinking, which triggered more thinking.

I began to love the process of tracking backwards. As this tracking process grew more refined, I began to notice that my thinking, depending on where it landed, would produce emo-tions. For example, if my thinking went into the future and started imagining possible negative outcomes, I would experi-ence a whirling sensation in my belly, which I labeled anxiety.

Or if it moved into the past, focusing on, for example, a memory of a loss, something gone missing, I found myself in the emotion of sadness.

The process became very interesting to me. When I arrived home after the retreat it became a technique that I continue to practice. I began to notice that when I was lost in thought I was able to track myself back to the moment. It was training me to witness and observe rather than to get caught up in the thought of the moment.

Our natural state is calm. At the center of who we truly are there is a peaceful presence. This presence is joyful, is loving, is creative.

The world calls us out from inside, In-Here. We exteriorize as we participate with action. We begin to identify with Out-There. We define ourselves as the roles we assume, the actions we take, the results we produce. We convince ourselves we are what we have and what we do. We get fooled into thinking we are our job, our gender, or sexual orientation. We identify with the size and shape of our bodies, our bank account, etc. We start to believe that what we think about this world is truth.

We forget where we come from.

We come from inside and from there we express into the world. Our expression is continually changing, yet the source of our expression is constant.

Why am I telling you this?

Because one of the things we're all here to discover in this Calm Down Lift Up process is that we are more than we think we are. We are not the circumstances we find ourselves in or the negativity we experience. There's something greater than all of us that is breathing us. Some people call it God. Some people called it the Divine. Some call it Soul, Atman, Allah. Those are just words. Words are the map, not the terrain. It doesn't matter what you call it as long as you know what it is. Let's call it the Magnificent Mystery.

The Magnificent Mystery is that which breathes us all. It animates our form. As Einstein proved, energy can neither be created nor destroyed. Thus, when this body dies, this mysterious energy still exists. It comes in on the breath, an inhale animating the body. We call that birth. It leaves on an exhale. We call that death.

2. You Are Not Alone

I took a deep breath and listened to the old bray
of my heart: I am, I am, I am.

Sylvia Plath

ↀↀↀ

You are much greater than your mind; more expansive than your emotions allow. You exist far beyond the body. Huh? Let's do an experiment.

Notice your body sitting on the chair, couch, lying on the bed. Become aware of your body. Invite your body to relax.

Shift your attention to the emotions. What are you experiencing? Agitation? Anger? Happiness? Peace? Anxiety? Sadness? Joy? What do you notice? Take a breath and allow the emotions to calm.

Move your attention and become aware of your thoughts. Notice your thoughts as they come and go. Take another breath and invite your thoughts to quiet.

Come with me on this one. I'm going to ask you a question. Take your time and let the response come to you.

Ask yourself: Who is the one doing all of that? Who is the one relaxing the body, calming the emotions, quieting the mind?

Take a moment to stop. Close your eyes. You may want to place a hand over your heart center, take an easy breath, and listen within for a response. Just close your eyes and open your ears and notice what shows up.

What is it for you? Who is the one observing?

When I do this in a workshop, the answer I most often hear is, "*I* am."

Well, who is this "I" that is noticing?

It couldn't be your body, your emotions, or your mind since whatever it is was *noticing* the body, mind and emotions. So, what is it that is noticing, that is aware, that pays attention, observes?

This I is not your ego, it is not your identity, it is not your personality, for this observing I can witness all of that. This I is greater than any of that. This is the I that says, I AM. I AM is the source of your creativity. I AM is Home.

You don't have to agree or disagree with me. I'm just asking you to sit with this and wonder about this I AM that notices — that has awareness — that is awareness. What is the source of that which pays attention, notices, is aware, observes and is witness to the experience of your life?

What if you turned your attention to that which is paying attention?

Mysterious?

Yes, and no. It is what some call the Soul, others call the Witness, and others call the Divine or Spirit. It doesn't care what you call it. (Just don't call It late for dinner.) This Something is the Magnificent Mystery of Life Itself. That which is Greater. The Source that breathes us ALL.

Have you noticed that you are not breathing you? The Spirit comes in on our breath. Even if you try to hold your breath, you cannot stop it from breathing you.

If it weren't for our breath, this body, mind and emotions, the package the breath animates, would not exist. We are not the package, though many of us have been distracted by identifying as the package. What great news for we know how limited this package is.

The you that exists beyond the body, mind and emotions is the one who brought quiet to the mind, calmed the emotions and relaxed the body. When we allow ourselves to lift up into our natural state of calm presence, our mind is open and available to inspiration and creativity.

Yet we live in a body, have a mind and emotions, and they will begin to activate again. This is what it is to be embodied. The mind starts to think about tomorrow. The emotions get agitated. The body wants to get up and get going. This comes with having a body and being human. When we move our focus back into the world, we fall into our humanity.

When we get riled up, we have a choice. We can choose to calm down instead of reacting to our upset. We can choose instead to respond by bringing ourselves to a place of peace.

Learning how to Calm Down and Lift Up is essential if we want to make good use of the package we come in. When we calm down, we have a sense of lifting and expanding. And in this expansion, we open to spiritual intelligence and wisdom. We open to That Which Notices.

This is your partner in life.

You are not doing this alone.

What a relief.

This awareness can transform your life.

This book will show you how.

3. Calming Crazy Brain

When we have inner peace, we can be
at peace with those around us.

The Dalai Lama

༚

Eek, that was scary! My computer just crashed to the ground. I am in a cabin, retreating from internet and cellular service so I can move this book to completion. I set the computer down on a footstool and walk away. Suddenly there is this LOUD NOISE. My mind recognizes it as the computer and I run to see if it has shattered.

I put the computer in my lap and here I am typing to make sure it is working. It seems there are no broken bones. Nothing to do but take a big breath. Be thankful. And, moving forward, to choose to be more careful about where and how I set my laptop down.

The sound disturbed my tranquility and called me to attention. There has been a break in transparency. It is as if I am tooling along the road and suddenly the tire blows. What that means is that the direction I thought I am going in is thwarted. Here I am making myself a cup of tea when BAM! Loud noise. Oh NO!

When there is a breakdown we often get upset. Fear and upset are natural when something unexpected happens. Upset is a normal reaction. It is appropriate for me to be afraid when my tire blows and I'm in the middle lane going 60mph. Fear is a call to action. The fear calls me alert and helps me get to the shoulder safely. Once I am on the shoulder, however, I need to engage my creativity in order to figure out how to get back into action.

Imagine the doorbell rings and the dog runs barking to the door. He sees through the window that it is friend and not foe. The hair on his neck lies down and his tail begins to wag. After greeting the visitor, he retreats to the pool of sunlight where he had been resting. He has calmed down from the disturbance caused by the ringing bell. He goes back to his nap.

Life is like that. Something is always happening. We get aroused. Fear is calling us alert, pay attention, something is happening other than planned. Like the dog running to the door checking out if there is a threat.

This was good when we were walking on the savanna with a pointy stick as our only company. There was a sound in the bushes and the mind ran into wondering, What does it mean? What do I do? This is the gift of a human brain. Referencing the past, we decide if the sound means there is something in the bushes about to eat us. Or if not, perhaps we can eat it. Hmmm, what do I do? Run or charge?

Useful for all these thousands of years, for here we are — still roaming planet Earth in our caveman/cavewoman bodies. Only now we have more than a pointy stick for company.

We no longer need to move into alert awareness accessing what is in the bushes every time something happens other than expected. We have evolved past our wiring for merely flight-or-fight reactivity. Our human consciousness has advanced beyond the package it walks around in.

The dog quiets down after arousal. In his resting state the adrenal rush that dumped adrenaline (epinephrine) into his blood stream has time to dissipate so he can come back to equilibrium. Yet it seems we human animals have lost the skill of calming down. We are so constantly bombarded with something or someone trying to get our attention that we become continuously aroused. There is no lying down in that spot of sunlight for a pause. There are emails to answer, deadlines to meet, children to carpool and ...

When we are so driven from without, we lose access to the space of calm that holds the wisdom within. We disconnect from the source of our well-being. Our lives become like a dog tethered to the tree - lots of barking, yet going nowhere. The brain is triggered into fear-based survival thinking, throwing us into the Hamster Wheel of Hades, sending us running around and around, going nowhere. We end up with a bad case of what I affectionately call Crazy Brain.

I remember a time after a particularly challenging break-up/breakdown, running around the hamster wheel of my Crazy Brain in an attempt to figure out what had happened. The truth was the relationship was over, yet I couldn't make my brain stop thinking about it. The tire had blown. He had gotten out of the car and walked away. I was on the side of the road. Some part of me imagined that if I could just figure out why that would be useful. Not. Thinking about his thinking triggered more of my thinking. Going nowhere fast. And then what? Nothing. Over is over.

Have you ever noticed our thoughts are like rabbits? They get active, make babies and more babies. Thinking about thinking about thinking, producing more thinking. A thought storm pulling us out of our calm center. The next thing you know, you're in Crazy Brain and have lost connection to your peace and well-being.

Well, I finally got a grip, got the tire changed and merged back into the flow of my life. Something happened. Life is like that. Now what?

I imagine there are few, if any of us, that enjoy the experience of investing in something that turns out not to reap a reward. Wallowing in our thinking about what happened won't change the outcome. There is nothing we can do about the past other than learn from it. Hanging out in I wish I would have/could have/should have reaps no positive reward. There is no 'interest' generated from that kind of thinking. No increase, no growth, no positive bottom line. There is loss. Loss of calm, peace, self-trust and opportunities to learn to do better next time.

Thinking about the past is very tempting. Wondering about how it is I got to here. And that is useful until it is no longer useful. The power is in now. Now what? What now? What did I learn and how can I use it to create more of what I want? Who do I want to BE-come, and where do I place my focus to foster that outcome?

This is a pivotal moment in our lives; a moment of choice we get presented with continuously. Where are we going to place our focus? In what is no longer, what is in the past? In what hasn't yet occurred, in the future? Or are we willing to call ourselves present to here and now and live from this moment, and now this one, and now this one?

What I have realized after a lifetime of choosing (or not choosing) the peace that is always present is that it is the fear of not knowing that has me running away from this moment. I see it in myself and I see it in the people I work with. Knowing we don't know can lead to anxiety unless we learn to calm ourselves in the face of the unknown.

When I find myself scurrying into the future trying to figure out what to do, I repeat to myself what Socrates said, "I am wise because I know I do not know." In doing so, I find myself quieting down and listening for the wisdom in the not knowing. I stop pretending I know what I do not know. The mind stops judging and the door to wisdom opens.

We all have access to wisdom. Wisdom is sourced from someplace other than the Crazy Brain. Wisdom comes from a quiet peace that is always present and available to us.

Learning to listen to the quiet within, instead of the frantic Crazy Brain, is an investment I encourage. It is one that will reap a bountiful harvest allowing access to inner wisdom. From this place you will be guided as to how to make use of the resources on hand, thus growing a more abundant future.

We, as humans, are gifted with imagination, the source of our creativity. We are the only animals that reference experiences from the past and project them into the future. We then embellish, tweak and create something new. This is a gift that has served us in inventing our current physical reality. It's why we have marvels that didn't exist even a hundred years ago. Like that thing I was typing upon. The one that fell to the floor and interrupted my Zen moment of tea.

4. The Mind is a Meaning Making Machine

In the absence of information,

we make things up.

Julio Olalla

ॐ

Notice I checked to see if my computer had shattered. Computers don't shatter falling from a height of six inches. My brain made that up. I heard a sound and my brain, which is a search engine, began looking for outcomes that matched that horrific sound. Looking in the reference files of the past it presented me with an image of a shattered computer.

As no damage was done as evidenced by the current reality of my typing, my brain had made a mistake. What I thought was true was in fact not true. My brain lied to me. Yours lies to you, too. It doesn't do this to hurt you. It is just doing its job. The mind is a meaning making machine. It makes stuff up all the time.

Now for a newsflash: You are not your brain. You are not your thoughts. You are not your imagination nor your emotions. You are much more than all of that. You are the one using this package that includes a mind, body, emotions, and more, to have the experience of life.

When you learn to calm the package, which is designed to get upset, you can use the mind as it was designed. Seeing possibility while simultaneously referencing the past. Designing action in the present in order to create something new.

This is the creative human, using circumstances to serve innovation, designing something even better than before. Like computers that can slip off a footstool and fall to the floor! Like footstools, and down pillows and sleeper sofas and cooked food!

Culinary anthropologists have a theory. They assess that back in the day when our ancestors were eating meat raw, there was a forest fire. The animals fled for safety leaving the burnt forest uninhabited by wildlife. Humans scouring for something to eat came across a carcass that had been burned by the fire. A hungry somebody reached down and ripped off some meat. Shoving it in her mouth she began to chew. Hmmm, easier to chew. Tasty too! Thus, humans designed a way to make use of fire to cook meat.

This is the human brain on creativity. We are resourceful, resilient, innovative and inventive. The way to access these gifts is by calming down so we can hear our creativity speaking.

NOW A STORY

Coming down for coffee one morning, I approached the sink and noticed this dark brown thing. As the brain sees what is familiar, I thought at first it was a browned outer lettuce leaf. Yet, that did not match reality. I didn't leave lettuce in my sink. Also, there was no way it would turn that color brown overnight if I had.

Then I saw a foot.

Now the mind guessed it was a frog. I have had a little frog in the house in the past. If it was a frog, it was the biggest frog I have ever seen up close.

The foot began to move. Just a little. And then my eyes began to see what was real. It was a bat. Asleep in the sink.

That was unexpected and I had an EEK moment! I quieted my mind with my breath. I became still and empty. In the emptiness a plan for action was revealed. It was as if the top of my head opened up and in came an idea. I was inspired.

The bat was resting on the wire tray I have at the bottom of the sink, which protects the finish. I gently placed a dishcloth over the bat. Even more gently I picked the tray up with the wrapped bat. I then took it out the door that I had already opened. Tenderly setting the tray down, I tipped it, removed the cloth and walked away (fast).

Returning to my house I periodically peeked out at the bat. It lay there for quite some time. Finally, I looked and discovered it was gone.

Bye, bye bat.

Creepy.

So, what's the point?

Screaming and throwing things at the bat would not have been helpful. It most likely would have provoked my worst fear in coming true: bat flying around my house and bombing my head, like a scene from Hitchcock's *The Birds.*

We usually make poor decisions when acting from upset.

Instead of panic, I quieted and listened for a solution to my problem. I just waited for insight to reveal itself. And it did.

If *I* can stay calm with a bat asleep in my sink, you can learn to calm down as well. Trust me, if *I* can do it, anyone can.

There is an interesting term from the field of neuroscience called *attention density.* It is a term for focusing concentration. What it means is that wherever you place your attention is where neural tissue grows.

Thus, if you have been focusing your attention on disturbance when things go other than planned, you may have unwittingly fostered growth of neural tissue that leads you to be easily upset. On the other hand, if you choose to focus your attention on calming down when life is upsetting, you will grow neural tissue that fosters peace, equanimity and ease. More neural tissue, easier, more intensive firing. If you want to get better at creating calm, make calming down when disturbed a practice. Neurons that promote peaceful states will literally grow.

Why should you care? Most people enjoy getting upset. Who's to blame for this fix I'm in?! Watching the CBN (Constantly Bad News) feeding the fixation on disturbance. Fueling the hamster on the wheel, which begins to run faster and faster.

Please note, the pursuit of calm isn't about making every single moment of existence perfectly tranquil. Instead it is a process of aliveness. Using irritation as a call to creative action, trusting you can handle whatever is put before you.

My point of view is that creativity is more fun than upset. Joy is a delightful place to live. Innovation may spark invention that could lead to a better world for thee and also for me.

Why would the effort to change your brain be worth it to you? You tell me. Because if you don't want to live in peace, creativity and joy there is nothing I can say that is going to make a difference. You have to choose it for yourself. You have to be willing to learn. And learning takes practice, repetition, drifting off course and getting back on again. Over and over and over again.

As you can see from the bat story, staying calm allowed me to be present, allowing something greater to come to me. It truly felt as if I was given the bat removal idea from something greater than my usual thinking mind. Inspiration.

Inspiration comes from a place deeper than thought. It comes when you have quieted, calmed and opened. It comes from spiritual intelligence.

There was joy as well as peace as I let creativity move me into action. I was excited to witness my plan in action. It was delightful to see the process unfold so beautifully.

ANOTHER STORY

I was working at my computer. I had a bath running. I decided to light a candle. I threw the match in the wastebasket after making sure it was out. Back to work I went until I noticed flames billowing out the basket. I picked up the basket and began to walk to the bathroom intending on tossing it into the tub. Quick creative action.

The only thing is it didn't work. Drat. As I walked the flames were driven towards me by the wind created by my movement. Creativity stepped in again and I observed myself make a 180°. Walking backward to the tub I tossed the basket into the water.

Voila! Crisis averted.

I am more effective when I stay calm and engaged rather than delaying the process by arguing with reality. In these two situations I did not have the luxury of time. Thus, the creative brain (the higher brain, the one us humans get to enjoy) kicked into gear and found an inventive solution to my problem.

We are amazingly resourceful. We can handle whatever circumstances arise. All we have to do is learn to Calm Down and Lift Up to our creative, resilient, resourceful brain.

Human beings are learning machines as well. Story number two has led me to create a habit of making sure matches are out by wetting the tip. I choose to learn from my experiences so I can create new behavior in the future. Behavior that serves me better and doesn't burn my house down.

In story number one, I had a pest control guy see if there was a nest of bats in my home. He also checked for holes where the bat might have snuck in. All was well, thus I concluded the hairy thing with wings followed me into the house the night before. I didn't see him. Since they are silent when they fly, I also didn't hear him.

I really have no idea how he got into my house or why he was asleep in my sink, and the mind wants to make up something, so that is my story. I may as well make it a pleasing tale.

Using the brain to make stuff up that is pleasant, uplifting or motivational, well, is kinda intelligent.

ঽ ৫ ঽ ৬ ঽ ৫

RX: Do This — Change Your Mind for the Good

(RX is an abbreviation for the Latin word "recipere" or "recipe" used here as a prescription for well-being)

- Here is something for you to begin to pay attention to: your thinking

- Thinking stimulates most of our feelings. When you feel upset turn your attention to your thinking. Tune into what is going on in there. If you are indulging in 'it is going to eat me' thoughts, you have my permission to change your mind. There is not much in our lives that warrants an 'it is going to eat me' panic attack.

- Future thinking is about fantasy. It's not real. Since the mind loves to make things up, make something up that feels good and is useful

- Play. Have fun. Win in your fantasies.

- Some people like to journal insights and shifts in perspective. I personally find this to be valuable. I am often surprised at what I wrote when I reread my notes. When we are in learning mode we are in conversation with our spiritual intelligence. My suggestion is to take notes. (Or not. You choose. There is no right or wrong way. Do what works best for you.)

5. Peace is Powerful

Nothing can bring you peace but yourself.

Ralph Waldo Emerson

꼴

The mind is an amazing gift of our human package. And it can also get us into trouble. Such as imagining a dreadful future when there's nothing going on but a scratch at the door. A scratch caused by a branch falling off a tree in a storm. Now the mind imagines something outside that wants to hurt you, some slimy thing from the depths.

Whoops. That was me when I was a little girl. One day in 5th grade we were shown a movie about spiders. They projected the images on a giant sheet on the wall of the cafeteria. The spiders were enormous. For nights, months, I was scared to fall asleep. I terrified myself by imagining a black widow spider crawling up my bed skirt. The movie told me a bite would kill me. I had no idea my mind was making me crazy. I would fall into a restless sleep and inevitably have a nightmare. Gratefully I grew out of it. It was tough.

It took longer to grow out of the pattern of scaring *myself.* My mind can be quick to imagine the sky is falling. Maybe it all stemmed from that movie about spiders. It doesn't matter. These patterns get conditioned from someplace. Perhaps I could say, mis-conditioned, for we are conditioned into not seeing what is true.

Every culture gives an explanation for everything. We grow up in language. Language creates our reality. We live in stories, rituals, protocols and rules.

Perhaps you were told there was a tooth fairy when you were a child. Dutifully you placed your tooth, the one that had ached for days and had finally been freed, under your pillow. Scrambling under the covers, eager to get to sleep so you could awake the next day and receive a reward. The tooth will have changed shape. For me it was changed into a quarter, for some it was candy. What did you find under the pillow? Or were there no tooth fairies in your childhood?

We accepted what we were told. The big people were like gods to us. Yet now that we are the big people, we know that not everything we were told and accepted was true. There is no tooth fairy. Well, not in my house. It was my dad. And guess what else? The world is no longer flat. It never was. Oh, you already know that.

It is part of our human journey to misunderstand reality, for the mind to run interference and distort things. Like imagining computers shattered when it was just a loud sound. The mind isn't doing it on purpose, it is just how it has been programmed. It hears a sound and begins a search, *What does this mean? What do I do?* It searches all the experiences, stories, data it has been fed, and it will produce an interpretation based on how it has been wired.

The good news is we don't have to be victims to our thinking. We can get a grip and take dominion by not taking our negative thinking so seriously. We don't have to get upset because we're upset.

Peace is here now. Peace is always present. When I'm not at peace I'm not present in the moment. I can check my thinking and see if I've bought into some version of reality that isn't fitting my experience. I can challenge myself with a question, *Is it true?* Is the meaning I am assigning to what is happening actually true? Most of the time it is a projection from the data banks of the past, the interpretation of reality that has become habitual in the way we make meaning of our lives.

I can also look and see if I have allowed my brain to take me into the future or the past. Neither one exists. All that is, is *here and now.* Nowhere to go, nothing to do. Nowhere is Now Here. Choosing to come present is powerful. From here, now, I can make choices and take actions to produce a preferred result, utilizing the beauty of being human with this amazing mind I have been given. Our human design allows us to live by design.

Calming down, coming present, is one of the most important skills we can learn. When I am calm, when I am at peace, there is an intelligence that is beyond the mind. This intelligence serves me in dealing with whatever circumstances I find myself. In the creative response there is a joy of aliveness that is the gift of our humanity.

Peace is powerful. We call ourselves present to the presence. We Calm Down to Lift Up into our greatest self. From here, we can do our best work and make a positive difference to our lives and to our world.

NOW A STORY

When I do BreathWork events, I use this silly looking karaoke-type machine. It amplifies my voice and amps up the music from my playlist. I was about to facilitate a group. I was all set and guess what? The karaoke machine contraption didn't work.

There was no power going into the unit. It wasn't the outlet — the outlet was sending juice. The machine was dead. How did that happen?

Life doing what it does. Another opportunity for me to access my creative brain and find another right answer to serve the moment, which I did.

The next day in Best Buy where I had purchased the unit, I asked a Geek from the Squad if he could assist me in discovering if the unit was permanently dead or just playing possum.

Thomas was kind and also very busy. I waited quite a while for him to return. I could have upset myself. I could have told myself the story that he was either ignoring me or choosing to purposely take care of others because he had something against short women. I could have fretted about wasting my time and thinking about everything else I could have been doing rather than waiting there doing nothing! On-and-on, imagining whatever, stirring myself up into a tizzy.

I didn't do that. That day I was at peace. I had left enough time in my day to handle this task and settled into the experience of waiting my turn.

. Forty-five minutes later, after thanking me for my kindness and patience, he was able to tell me my machine had died a quick and probably painless death due to shorting out and could not be revived. He then ran around the store doing whatever he could to help me find a solution to my problem, boosting my voice while amplifying music.

He was definitely acting above and beyond the call of duty, and with gratitude I told him so. He said it was due to my willingness to be patient with his delay in waiting on me.

Wow. An outer reward for patience. For me patience was its own reward.

Irritation with people has not been a successful strategy in my life. People do what they do even if I want them to be doing something else. Impatience with the process is as effective in changing my outer circumstances as is complaining about the weather. A useless investment of my energy and an experience that makes the moment (and me) less than lovely.

I told Thomas as such (in simpler words). He smiled as he continued to see if he could find some way to fix me up with sound support.

Although I didn't leave the store physically with anything more than my now officially useless karaoke machine, I did leave with a sense of gratitude for a deeper recognition that I AM the source of peace in my life.

Peace is sourced from the acceptance of what is. What is, is. That's it. Life is What Is. I get to live in the experience of how I choose to relate to What Is. Irritation and complaint contribute to againstness and upset. Acceptance fosters peace, and apparently, sometimes inspires others to be the best of themselves. Icing on the cake, and the cake is yummy all by itself.

P.S. I'm a person who is still in the classroom of learning to be patient with the process. This story is one of those moments that reminds me it is worth the practice.

※ ※ ※

Hmmm — Ponder This:

How are you creating disturbance in your life by arguing with What Is?

※ ※ ※

6. The Elephant and the Ant

Peace is the result of retraining your mind to process
life as it is, rather than as you think it should be.

Wayne W. Dyer

༄༅

Insanity is holding onto thinking that doesn't match real-ity. We then argue with reality because it doesn't look like our thinking. This is an attempt to control reality to make it look like what we want it to in our imagination.

Wrestling with reality is like an ant telling an elephant to get out of its way. There's no way the elephant is going to move. No matter how loud the ant yells, or how hard it stamps its tiny foot, how much it begs, pleads or flirts, the elephant is going to do whatever it wants to do. Elephants are like that.

The ant is doomed by holding on to thinking that doesn't match reality.

Squish.

So much for defying the reality we live in.

I have a friend who mentioned that the carpet in her home was dirty, even disgusting. She then told me she could live with it. She would just look elsewhere and ignore the reality of her dirty carpet.

When she told me her strategy for dealing with her condi-tions, I imagined she must rent. I figured she had a lousy landlord who refused to accommodate an upgrade.

Months later we're having lunch, and she referred to her property taxes. It dawned on me that she is the landlord. My brain wrinkled in wonder about complaining over something she can change.

Then I remembered that I am not unlike that. I was once in a relationship with a man who was consistently unkind to me; I didn't get new carpet either. I just pretended it wasn't happening. I looked someplace else thinking I could get the elephant to do what I wanted to do if only ...

It didn't.

That's insane!

And highly anxiety provoking.

The world (people, the polar icecaps ... my mother) does what it does. We are not in control. The Magnificent Mystery that breathes all of Life is in charge. If we don't like it, we suffer. If we argue with our circumstances we suffer. If we think we know better, we suffer.

Move! said the ant.

Splat.

Anxiety is a result of realizing that the world does what it does and we're not in control. We suffer when we grasp on to results that do not appear, holding onto thinking that doesn't match reality. We attempt control by pretending we can get an elephant to do our bidding, even though we know it ain't gonna happen.

The key is to be loving to the part that is anxious. It doesn't matter what you are thinking or feeling. Your concerns about the world's activities or elephants in the road are irrelevant. Take a few breaths; bring yourself to peace.

Loving is the antidote to disturbance. Bring your loving to the disturbance and it will calm. From calm you will discover you have the energy, insight, and wisdom to handle the situation. Including crossing over to the other side of the street, letting the elephant have his way.

ঽ ৫ ঽ ৬ ঽ ৫

RX: Do This — Love the Disturbance

- Allow yourself to feel the upset in your body.

- Comfort yourself with a gentle reminder that it is okay to be upset. Life is sometimes disturbing.

- Assure yourself, all is well. Take a breath.

7. FEAR and the Man Behind the Curtain

Don't worry about the world coming to an end today.
It's already tomorrow in Australia.

Charles Schultz

ॐ

Life does what it does. What you do with what life does is the experience you get to live in. Sometimes what we do is make things up. Sometimes what we make up frightens us. How do we scare ourselves?

Let's look at the word FEAR:

F E A R

Fantasized

Expectations

Appearing

Real

Fantasized **E**xpectations **A**ppearing **R**eal

Imagining your imminent demise!

No, no, no, don't follow the Yellow Brick Road. There is a belching head of fire at the end of the road. If that doesn't get you, the Wicked Witch of the West will! Go back where you came from.

Don't look at the man behind the curtain. Ignore him. No, no, no, keep focused on the belching flames coming out of the floating head. Scaring you into inaction. Shutting you down. Terrified to take a step forward in your life.

We forget that fear is a survival mechanism telling us we've not been here before. It is saying, *pay attention.* That's all it is. This call to attention doesn't say run back into your comfort zone, lock the doors and tuck-in with the covers over your head. It is calling you alert, telling you that you are in new territory, reminding you to bring all your resources to bear. Pay attention. Come present. Presence is powerful.

There is FEAR, as in a saber-tooth tiger is going to eat me if I don't get my butt up this tree. Then there is fear, as in I'm imagining the sky is falling and I am freaking out that my life is falling apart. The first fear got us this far in our evolution. The second one drives us bananas.

Fear is your ally when you are in new territory. This intrinsic survival mechanism is still operating on a basic level even though we are rarely, if ever, in life-threatening circumstances. When we step out of our comfort zone, when something unexpected occurs, a part of us becomes alert and attentive.

When we don't take action the energy of alertness turns into what we call fear. Instead of engaging in positive ways towards creating something *next,* we get stuck in fantasies of doom and gloom.

Have you ever paused to notice that the sensation of fear in the body is very similar to excitement? Consider the whirling in the belly, the sense of anticipation due to something happening. The difference between fear and excitement is focus. When we imagine a negative outcome, we feel frightened. When we imagine a positive outcome, we feel excited.

Early in my life, when I was single, I received a call from my mother after not hearing from me, according to her, for too long. She exclaimed, "I was so worried about you living alone. I didn't know if you had died and no one would find out until the body began to stink!" I'm not kidding. This happened.

Worry is how we run away from facing the fear. We worry that something is going to go wrong. We believe worrying is doing something. In truth, it is a distraction from creativity. If we are focusing on what might go wrong, we are not tending to the questions: *What does this mean?* and *What do I do?* Choosing what to DO is key. Action is what you contribute to the creative process while life is doing what it does. It's navigating by putting your rudder into the water. Showing up and participating.

In the movie *The Wizard of Oz,* the wizard seemed a lot scarier projected as Bigger than Reality onto the screen in the great room. That is what worry and fear do when we are stuck in them. They make what is challenging seem bigger than is manageable by any mere mortal.

Often people scare themselves into inaction because there are no guarantees. If I take an action, I will produce a result. What if I don't like the result I produce? What if I don't like the result someone else produces?

What if ... Eek! Oh, No! Now we are running around the *what ifs* in our thinking and nothing is really going on.

We may get married and then divorce. We may plan a vacation in a warm place for some sun and end up with a week of rain and storms. We may finally get to Oz only to find out we need to come back with the broom of the Wicked Witch of the West in hand. Not at all what we had in mind when we started down the Yellow Brick Road.

It is important to honor the voices of worry and fear. They can be allies if we use them well. Turn instead and face the fear. Look at the Worst Possible Outcome and figure out what you would *do* if the Worst Occurred. You may surprise yourself with your resourcefulness. You may find that the Worst of All is just another bump in the road.

You may find the Wizard wasn't all that scary. He wasn't even a wizard. He was just an ordinary man.

I suggest you go ahead and look at the man behind the curtain. You will find the situation is much more manageable than your **F**antasized **E**xpectations **A**ppearing **R**eal are telling you.

What happens when you face your fears and let yourself feel your feelings? You open up a connection with your creativity. Once that door opens you are able to assess the situation and get innovative about solving it.

Here is what a dialog with Worry might sound like:

Worry: I am worried we might not make it. I'm afraid we'll get divorced.

You: And then what?

Worry: We'll have to sell the house and move.

You: And then what?

Worry: I'd probably move to California, to be closer to my friends.

You: And then what?

Worry: I'll ask Josie if I can stay with her until I get things sorted out.

You: And then what?

Worry: I'll have to set myself up for income.

You: And then what?

Worry: I know lots of folks. I have a lot of contacts.

You: And then what?

Worry: I guess I'd get my own place once I have work in place and start over.

You: And then what?

Worry: By then I imagine my heart will have healed some.

You: And then what?

Worry: At some point I'd start dating again.

You: And then what?

Worry: I don't know. I guess I'll find out.

You: Do you think you'll be okay?

Worry: I imagine so.

You: What do you really want?

Worry: Even though I know I'll be okay, I prefer to make my marriage work.

You: How can you help create that?

Worry: I'm going to talk to my husband this weekend and tell him how much he means to me.

Can you see how you have liberated all sorts of energy that was tied up in worry? You have faced your fear and realized that even though you would not prefer that path, you will be okay. Now you can invest that energy into action to support what you really want. Way to go! You have empowered yourself yet again, by attending to your attention, directing your focus and taking action.

Which approach will serve you best? Worry and focus on the worst possible outcome or facing your fears, uncovering your concerns and choosing action to support what you want?

Go ahead. Do look at the man behind the curtain. Face what it is that is frightening you. You may surprise yourself and may discover *you* are the wizard who can make things happen.

Ahhh, that's better. You can now relax into your creativity, trusting that all is well.

ॺ ॺ ॺ ॺ ॺ ॺ

RX: Do This — Pull Back the Curtain

- Pay attention to your thinking. Notice when you are telling yourself scary stories about the future that have no substance. Just a floating head projected on a screen with belching fire for special effects.

- Notice how you scare yourself into inaction.

- Might it be just smoke and pretense?

- Pretend the worst is what is. What are you going to do about it?

- *Now what?*

- Optional: You may want to journal what you discover.

8. Mitigating a Thought Storm

If you know you are not the mind, then what difference does it make if it's busy or quiet? You are not the mind.

Nisargadatta Maharaj

༄

I'm wondering, what do you do when there's a storm? Be it a blizzard or thunderstorm replete with lightning and pouring rain. Perhaps there is wind howling, gusting up to 40 miles or more an hour.

I understand there are people who make a sport of chasing storms. Are you one of those people who follows the storm, getting involved at the edges, risking imminent danger? Or are you, like most of us, someone who stays home, tucked in under a throw blanket, comfortable in front of a warm fire, drinking tea as the wind howls outside your window?

I love watching storms from inside my cozy house, especially thunderstorms. All the rumbling, the flashes of light, the big bang overhead. Rain pounding against my windows. Unless I must, I do not venture outdoors.

Yet, most of us hang out in the whirling fury of thought storms. Swept up in the mind's ongoing battle with itself.

"Go left!" it cries.

"No, go right."

"But if I go right, I might fall off the cliff."

"Well, then, go up."

"No, I'll go down."

"You should know how to do this already!"

"Are we there yet?"

"You shouldn't have done that!"

"Who do they think they are?"

"Well, maybe it was my fault."

"Oh no, not that again."

The mind loves to talk to itself. It is no fun when I allow myself to be tempted into the storm, for indeed, I suffer from my thinking.

NOW A STORY

Imagine you are in a train station. A train pulls up. You don't know where it is going. You get on. You find out upon arrival it was going to hell. Fortunately for you, you find your way back to the train station.

Trains come and trains go. Leaving from here and going to there. You get on another train and find out it is the same line as the one before. You end up in hell.

Luckily you find yourself back in the train station. Now you realize paying attention is a good idea. You tell yourself not to get on a train unless it is going somewhere you want to go.

You wait. You are quiet. There is nothing going on. Trains come and trains go. You realize you don't have to go anywhere. Where you are is just fine.

The thoughts that run around our head are like those trains. Many take us places we'd prefer not to go. We end up in a sort of hell. The Hamster Wheel of Hades. Miserable and suffering because we got on the train of our thoughts. By now you'd guess we'd know better. Trains come and trains go. Most are going nowhere fast. We don't have to get on. We can stand in stillness and quiet at the station, the noise of the moving train in the background. We don't have to get on.

And if, per chance, we find ourselves on a train going to hell, we can get off.

Often what we perceive is a reflection of the quality of the thoughts in our head. If in a crappy mood, the dishes in the sink are irritating. If in a good mood, the dishes in the sink are put in the dishwasher with a smile. It's not about the dishes, is it?

A client came in upset about her boyfriend. She was spinning and spinning. Her spinning created more spinning while she was getting more and more upset. At our previous meeting she was blissed out because he was the best thing that had ever happened in her life. I don't think the boyfriend changed that much in two weeks. How she was filtering their relationship was what was disturbing her. How dare he leave the dishes in the sink, she asks herself, and on the train to hell she goes.

Thinking is like peristalsis (look it up) of the brain. Just let it do what it needs to do. It will clear up on its own. Too often we hang out in the experience, allowing our thinking about what happened disturb us even more. When the mind is not managed, we tend to suffer. Just let it all go and move on to *next*.

Recently my mind was doing battle with itself. Something innocuous had happened, and for whatever reason, my mind was off and running in a conversation about nothing. Because the topic had no real relevance to my life, it was fascinating to observe. As I noticed the gabfest, I realized this happens all the time. The mind never stops talking to itself. No matter how many times I watch my breath or how much I meditate, the mind keeps talking.

What does change is my relationship to all the noise. I develop my ability to either back off and observe (thus not getting swept into the storm) or to not pay attention at all. This becomes a blessing in my life. Holding quiet in the midst of the chaos of stormy thinking.

My mind is the noisiest when I'm stepping outside my comfort zone into something new. Eek — Oh boy — Oh No — Wow! Back-and-forth between fear and excitement. My choice is to breathe-in and breathe-out, take the next step, tune into any part of the message that might be useful, and leave the rest alone.

My client realized this is what provoked the thought storm she had brought into our session. She had just become engaged. Eek, Oh Boy, I am getting married!

If you find yourself in hell, get off the train. If you get tempted out in the storm, turn around, go back to the station and take yourself Home.

9. White-It-Out

We do not need magic to change the world,
we carry all the power we need inside ourselves
already: we have the power to imagine better.

J. K. Rowling

☙❧

Being human and all, I bet you too sometimes get on the thought train to hell. Not fun. It happens to all of us every now and again. Sometimes the mind gets hold of a thought and chews on it like a dog with a bone, even though the bone is rotten, full of maggots and eventually will make you sick. Yuck.

I had a client who had just gotten engaged. He was mostly excited about their future together, except at those times when his mind kept recalling where former relationships hadn't worked out. He would have these thoughts and then doubt would grip him in the belly and throw him around the room. Ow.

I taught him the White-It-Out Method. The moment you catch the negative thought rearing its ugly head, envision having a giant jar of white-out and painting over the thought, creating a clean, white board. Then write on the board something you'd *prefer* to focus upon.

For example, my client was scaring himself by imagining his soon-to-be wife turning into his no-longer-wife along with all the expenses that accompany a divorce. Not a motivating experience when one is planning a wedding. He practiced the White-It-Out Method and instead of focusing on relationship doom, he took a moment to remind himself, that was then, and this is now. He then took a giant white-out brush and made the sad ending disappear replacing it with a story of happiness and relationship fulfillment. Ahhh, much better.

It sounds simple, yes? Too simple? No. The brain is plastic and can be rewired. Consistent focus will change the structure of the brain. Focus on what you want and the brain will rewire itself to accommodate your desire. For example, focusing on gratitude actually grows more brain matter that associates to the experience of gratitude. (By the way, the brain will also do this when we focus on what we don't want. I suggest we all take charge of our focus.)

I encourage you to try this if you find you have a thought habit you'd like to change. With practice, you'll find yourself easily shifting to imagining what you really want. Focusing on what you want feels GOOD!

Not only will you WIN in your own fantasies, you'll actually be changing your brain to support you in more easily creating what you want!

10. Turning Worry to Wonder

My life has been filled with terrible misfortune;
most of which never happened.

Michel Montaigne

༺༻

There are many expressions representing the uselessness of worry. One is that it is a misuse of the imagination. Another is that it is praying for something you don't want. Yet most folks think worry is beneficial. Will Rogers is quoted as saying, "I know worrying works, because none of the stuff I worried about ever happened." Of course, he was jesting. Yet many consider worry to be a rabbit foot keeping them out of harm's way.

It doesn't work like that. Worry freezes our brain. We stop thinking of creative solutions and get stuck in thinking about thinking about thinking about the future which isn't happening now. It sets our focus on a terrible outcome and then we believe fretting about it is going to make it work out. An attempt to control the uncontrollable future that isn't even here yet. Worry is another way to fuel your journey on the Hamster Wheel of Hades, destination nowhere.

One of my clients, who I adore, has the habit of beginning her sentences with *I worry about ___*. This happens many times during the course of her sharing about what has gone on for her leading up to our conversation. Then, as she is telling me about what she sees next, she begins with phrases like, *I worry ___. I worry about ___*, or *I worry that ___*.

We've played with choosing another approach. As with most long-term habits, it takes more than just a good idea to make a change. It takes repetition to make a positive difference.

The next time I heard her say, "I worry" I stopped her. "Let's say that sentence again. This time replace the word 'worry' with 'wonder.'"

This simple shift made a dramatic difference. Watch this:

I worry that my mom is living alone and may fall, and no one will know.

I wonder how I can support my mom in practicing her balancing exercises and remembering to wear her Life Alert necklace.

I worry that I ate too much last night.

I wonder how I can increase my exercise today and handle going off course last night.

I worry that my sister is drifting away and our relationship is eroding.

I wonder how I can nurture my connection with my sister and deepen the friendship I cherish.

Got it?

Worry does nothing other than promote more worry, fretting and stress. Worry fosters upset. Wonder leads to creativity. Wonder opens up to possibility and choices. Choices lead to action. Action leads to results. Results which can be fine-tuned with more action.

Worry never stopped anyone from falling down, from gaining weight, from eroding relationships. Yet there is evidence that participation in the process with intention to co-create a preferred outcome has a very high percentage of success.

I wonder how you will train yourself to stop worrying and choose wondering?

[P.S. To turbo-charge this process, practice the White-It-Out Method as well. White-out the worry image and then replace it with an image of a preferred outcome.]

TIME TO PAUSE

Turn your attention within.

Notice your breathing.

Observe what is present.

Take a conscious breath into your belly.

Exhale and continue.

11. Forgetting Everything is All Right

If you don't like what you are looking at
look someplace else.

John Morton

ॠ

Even if you cannot hear a sound, there is classical music playing in the room you are in. If you had an FM radio you could turn it on, dial into a classical music channel, and listen to what is being broadcast. The music is already playing. You are choosing to tune in.

Perhaps you have formatted your tuner to go there by pushing a button. I have that choice in my car. I can pre-select stations. These are programmed in for easy access. If I want to listen to something not programmed, I use the search feature for a new station.

Imagine thoughts are like radio waves. Present and not audible until you tune in to the station of choice. Perhaps you've made the station that broadcasts judgment and criticism your default. You have programmed yourself to listen to WJDG and all you hear is non-stop blabbering. Noise that sounds like nobody can ever do anything right, including you!

Out of all the choices of stations to tune in to, perhaps your favorite is WRRY. Oh, no! — what if this happens? If I fret enough maybe it won't happen. Eek-eek-eek, the sky is falling. This time, for sure!

Neither broadcast is soothing or is bringing you good cheer. Yet, it's what is playing on the radio, so you endure. Life is just like that you think. Bad news wherever you go!

We have forgotten that we're the ones that chose the default settings on the radio. Well, maybe we had a little help from the conditions we grew up with — our family, culture, school and more. All of which contribute to how our brain filters our circumstances. Then we forget. We forget there is a dial we can turn. We forget thinking is just the brain broadcasting. Just like the radio, not everything the announcer says is true or useful. Just like the radio, we can change the station.

When you catch yourself in Crazy Brain with steam coming out of your ears, or biting your fingernails, or eating more than your body needs, or ... turn your attention to your thoughts. Change your mind. Shift from the Crazy Brain station to something else.

How about WCLM? Something that calms and lifts.

An easy shift to calm is to focus on the breath.

- Begin by watching your breath.

- Shifting out of your head, feel your feet on the floor

- Let yourself drop into your body as you notice your chest cavity expanding and contracting with each inhale and exhale

- Allow yourself to find a place of stillness within

- Notice the quiet

- Be with the quiet until you recognize that Everything is All Right.

- You just forgot. Now you are remembering.

- Allow yourself to relax into peace as you calm down.

If you want everything to be even better than *all right* then put your *life is amusing glasses* on. Perhaps you can follow Marilyn vos Savant's lead, "At first, I only laughed at myself. Then I noticed that life itself is amusing. I've been in a generally good mood ever since."

NOW A STORY

I was facilitating a BreathWork event in Chicago. The attendant at the place I was renting told me they would open up at 12:20. Plenty of time for me to set up, as folks would begin to arrive at 12:45. I arrived at 12:20.

I found the door locked. No one was there.

No one answered when I called the venue. It was the only number I had.

I waited in my car as the damp, chilled January wind penetrated my bones. The first of the participants began gathering outside the venue. I met them and told them we had no entry. They were lovely. I, on the other hand, was on the verge of tears. I was listening to a station that was less than supportive.

Deciding to look for an alternative space, I saw that there was a public library a half block away. I talked my way into the lobby as the library opened at 1pm (the time my event was scheduled). I asked the guard if there was a room to rent. She didn't know but told me who I could talk to when the library opened. Well, that wasn't going to work.

Back on the street, I went into the restaurant next to the venue and asked if I could rent their banquet room. Nope.

Leaving the restaurant, I looked north and saw the Old Town School of Music. Guess where I went? All the dance studios were occupied. Besides, there was paperwork to fill out and that paperwork person didn't work on Sunday.

In the middle of all the outer chaos, including the part of me that wanted to cry, I realized at the center of it all I was calm. I was even having fun figuring it out. I had begun to listen to WCLM. I had surrendered. I had no control over the circumstances. I kept taking action with the intention of finding an alternative. There was nothing else I could have done. I gave it up (rather than gave up).

At 12:55 the attendant arrived with a hushed apology and opened the door. We scampered in, happy for a warm space.

It turned out *fine.* Everything was all right

No matter how it turned out I would have been fine. Here's what I mean by *fine.* At the core of me I am always fine. However life unfolds, I can guide myself to the place of peaceful calm that is at my center. A place similar to the still depths of the ocean, beneath the choppy, at times turbulent, surface.

It's just that we think it's not *fine*. The Misery Making Mechanism of the Mind focuses on the ever-moving surface of our lives. Recognizing it is not in control it gets upset by life's disturbances.

Circumstances change. The only thing in life that is constant is change. Yet there is a changeless state that is always present and is a resource for each of us.

Changing conditions are similar to the ocean surface, continuously moving. If we pay attention to life only at the surface of experience, we find ourselves bouncing around like a buoy floating on a choppy ocean: in disturbance. Instead, the anchor of the buoy is rooted into the bottom of the ocean: in stillness.

In any moment you could drop your awareness and attend to the stillness at the depth of you. You could do it now. Turn your attention to the still place inside of you. Some find closing their eyes helpful. Give yourself time to locate the stillness, the calm, the quiet within. Pay attention to it. Discover what happens. What do you notice?

For me, I find a space that is expanded, clear and free. I also discover the joy that is, just because I am. It isn't something learned. It isn't something created. It is something I turn my attention to and allow to come into awareness. It is always there.

Can you feel it? If not, pay attention until you do. It's a gift you give to yourself that has value beyond measure.

BreathWork helps us go to the place inside where it is all *fine* — regardless of circumstances. At the core of everything is a quiet stillness that is always *fine*. In the stillness the upset calms.

Ahh, big sigh.

Big Breath.

Life happens. It doesn't happen for a reason. Life is neutral. We make whatever happens good for us by how we engage. When we turn into WCLM we can find our way to our creativity and find another way to grow.

I have made WCLM a favorite on my programmed radio. On radio station WCLM, everything is alright, all right.

12. Oy to Joy

There is no doubt that creativity is the most important human resource of all.

Edward de Bono

भूॐ

Difficulties and obstacles in life are often blessings, for in reality we grow through adversity. As we turn stumbling blocks into steppingstones, energy is liberated, which can be used to create a life that is rich and satisfying. A useful wonder question: *What blessings are you living in now that are the consequences of difficulties?*

I am from New York, from a culture that says, *Oy,* as an exclamation in reaction to something going other than planned. Also spelled *oy vay, oy veh,* the expression may be translated as, *Oh, woe!* or *Woe is me!*

A bit ago, I heard myself say *Oy* aloud when something happened other than I planned. Hearing myself exclaim this tribal grunt made me smile, amused that this expression was alive in me.

A week later I heard myself mutter, *Oy,* again. I became curious as to what was fueling the automatic *Oy.* I began to see that it is what I say when there is an unexpected turn of events.

Oy!

And *now what?*

There is always *next.*

Oy ... *now what?*

Well, I love problem solving. When there is *Oy,* there is also the opportunity to do something. Find a possible solution to my problem and take action into that possibility. Fun!

Now when I hear myself declare in woe, *Oy,* I realize I'm on my way from *Oy* to JOY! Oh boy, there has to be a solution around here someplace! What can I create out of this?!

Oy to Joy.

Moving from seeing a problem to the fun of creating a solution.

NOW A STORY

A client came to me asking for help. Her husband had died, and her circumstances had led her to let go of her house and downsize. The project seemed daunting. Big Oy. Through our work, she turned the problem into a project.

At the conclusion of our time together she was full of excitement. Instead of being gripped with fear as she was when we first began to work, she was in full-out creative action mode updating her house for market, while planning to move into a lovely new community.

She was on fire with action and was grateful for her network of support and for the fun she was having finding creative ways to fix up her house for sale.

This widow, instead of feeling burdened by her loss, was embracing her circumstances as a doorway into the rest of her life.

She had moved from Oy to JOY!

Where would you like to place *your* focus? Oy or Joy? Can you turn a problem into creative joy by seeing the possibilities in the situation before you?

ॿ ౮ ౮ ౮ ॿ ౮

RX: Do This — Meditation — What If There is "No Problem to Solve?"

- What happens when you turn your attention to the quiet within and wonder ... what if there is *no problem to solve?*

- What goes away when the problem-solving part of the brain is asked to pause?

- What comes present to fill the space?

- Notice what is here when there is *no problem to solve.*

- From this place of *no problem to solve* what is true?

  * Gratitude to Loch Kelly for this inquiry.

13. Anxietment

Fear is excitement without the breath.

Fritz Pearls

ॐ

Anxietment is a state we humans go into when something NEW is about to happen. We fluctuate between fear (oh no — it will be bad!) and excitement (oh boy — it's going to be great!) I call it *anxietment.* If you think about it, fear and excitement feel similar in the body. The difference, as I have stated, is where we place our focus when facing the unknown — a negative outcome (anxiety) or a positive one (excitement).

Change is a life-happening experience. We either provoke change or it knocks at our door. Whenever we involve ourselves in a change process, we are vulnerable to the experience of *anxietment.* Change is a process of moving from where we are to where we want to be. That goal is outside our comfort zone, the zone of the familiar. To get there we must leave our comfort zone. By definition leaving the comfort zone is uncomfortable.

Once we step outside our comfort zone the body begins to send us extra energy so that we can pay attention and be alert as we move forward into uncharted territory. This energy is neutral. It's what we do with the energy that determines the experience we have. If I focus on the negative possibilities, I will scare myself, contract my body, and limit my breathing. This is often experienced as anxiety or fear.

If, on the other hand, I begin to feel that energy stirring, and I focus on moving my body, keeping my breath full, while concentrating on a successful outcome, I will find myself excited.

Depending upon where I place my focus, I can feel scared about the future, or I can get excited about the possible/probable outcomes. Clearly, where I place my focus determines my experience in the moment. Since I'd rather win in my own fantasies, and the future is still undetermined, I'd rather place my focus on the best possible outcome.

I, for one can shift between the two, thus my familiarity with what I have named *anxietment*. *Anxietment* is a moving back and forth between anxiety and fear. Anxiety when I land on negative future thinking, and excitement when I'm focused on a positive outcome.

NOW A STORY

I was sitting in the family waiting area for surgical patients at Northwestern Hospital. My then husband, now wusband, was in surgery. He was getting an upgrade for his left hip joint.

I had lots of energy moving, also known as emotions (energy in motion). I had my computer with me and decided to use the time and energy to write an article for my blog. While writing I had an awareness. When I focused on the fear of the worst outcome, which the doctor said was, well, death, I found myself quite anxious. Yet, when I focused on the best outcome, a pain free hip and more joy in living, I felt excited about what may come.

In that moment I began to laugh and realized that I was living in the energy field of *anxietment.* It's a combo package, part anxiety/part excitement.

After that it became a game. I would feel that familiar wave of nausea and rolling in my belly. I then took a peek inside, and voila! There was the scary story running around my Crazy Brain. Recognizing it was the Man Behind the Curtain messin' with me, I changed the film reel. Much better movie.

In the new movie I saw the doctor checking in. The surgery was a success!

I could hear music playing. I imagined dancing with my partner celebrating the pain-free joy of his new hip.

Cha-Cha-Cha.

Anxietment is a common occurrence when we have stepped outside our comfort zone. The best way to deal with it is to first recognize it, and name it. That in itself shifts it for me. Go ahead, say the word aloud. It is fun.

I'm feeling anxietment.

Speaking the word makes me smile. Smiling is lifting. Laughter too. Perhaps you could skip and laugh and smile and say, *I'm full of anxietment!* (Just sayin' maybe you could.)

Now take a breath, and say, *I'm excited because ___,* filling in the blank with something which would be joyful to experience.

ᘓ ᘔ ᘗ ᘘ ᘓ ᘔ

RX: Do This — Turning Eek to Oh Boy!

- Write down your vision of the positive outcome you see as possible.

- Breathe into this possibility.

- Is there an action you can take from here that might get you to there?

- Take that action.

- Perhaps choosing gratitude for the blessings *here and now* is the best next action.

14. Feeling Excited About Reality

*Your imagination is your preview of
life's coming attractions.*

Albert Einstein

༺ༀༀ༻

Not only is everything all right, everything is good and getting better. The blessings are abundant *here and now* and more are on the way. We potentiate the blessings with our participation and our focus.

Don't believe me? Put your *good-things-happening-glasses* on. Look past the superficial aspects of your life. Most people, when they look, can see the gifts of the hard times which serve as the classroom for growth and expansion.

We all suffer our minds. An untrained mind loves to complain. Training the mind entails purposefully sorting through the 4 million bits of data we receive in every moment. Our consciousness only processes about 2,000 of those bits. So what determines which bits of information we process and which bits are left out?

Our conditioning, experiences, socialization, and more, program our filtering. Thus, one experience, witnessed by several people will yield the same amount of interpretations. Each person will process their 2,000 bits and reach a particular conclusion. Since there are 4 million bits, it is unlikely any two people will reach the exact same conclusion.

A client was telling me about her husband who was in the process of recovering from surgery. According to the doctors, physical therapists and nurses, he was ahead of the healing curve and on the top side of speedy recovery. Alas, he saw only hardship, struggle and the inability to do squats at the same weight at the gym as he could just prior to surgery. According to his thinking, his body was healing too slowly. It may have served him to look through the eyes of his support team. He might have been able to calm down and experience his recovery process as the gift everyone else saw it was.

Calming down helps you change your brain, so it filters the events of your life as a gift. Thus, you see positive possibilities in what was previously called problems.

NOW A STORY

After returning from a trip to Cuba, a client reported having a very different experience of from that of her fiancé. The trip had them changing planes in Mexico. Upon arrival, they discovered they had to retrieve their bags and check in at a different terminal. The terminal was quite a distance considering they had bags to schlep. Once at the next terminal, they waited in line for over an hour in order to recheck their bags. When they finally got to the counter, they discovered one bag had gained weight from Chicago to Mexico. It was now overweight!

Her fiancé was fuming as he pulled out his credit card to pay for the overage only to find out his credit card was declined. They were sent to another line.

Meanwhile, friends they were traveling with were supplying the couple with margaritas. My client found the whole thing a comedy. Her fiancé, on the other hand, definitely did not. She knew they would end up where they were going eventually. She decided to enjoy the ride.

The power tools here are acceptance and humor. My client chose to have fun. This is really funny. I'm going to make this fun because there's nothing else to do. Within the constrictions of my circumstances I might as well lift up to humor and play with whatever has been put in my sandbox.

Negative doesn't mean bad. We make things bad by judging them, by the meaning we put on our circumstances. What is bad about a suitcase that gained weight in the baggage hold from Chicago to Mexico City? What is bad about waiting in line, or a declined credit card? Not bad, just not what was expected or anticipated. Perhaps negative, but not bad. So what? *Now what?*

One of my mentors would often remind me that I could go through life laughing or crying but go through life I will. A useful reminder. Circumstances may be out of my control, yet my attitude about my circumstances is my choice.

Attitude and actions. How we show up now influences later. My client saw the humor. How the heck did that bag gain weight? She moved to a place of calm playfulness. She also saw her fiancé as making his own choices. She didn't judge him for his choices. Being disturbed doesn't make it better.

Getting upset that he was upset would just produce more upset. She got to live in the pleasure of her own company. Additionally, as her calm, joy, peace and sense of play radiated and touched others, she was a calming influence on her partner. Even if he didn't know it!

Let's play with this some more. If you want, you could take your eyes from this page and scan your room. Notice what you notice. If you do that now you may learn from the experience. Go ahead. Scan your room.

Now, look again, this time with the intention of finding all the red in the room.

What did you notice? Most folks report seeing more red than before as that was their choice of focus. It is a "seek and ye shall find" kinda thing.

The red was always there.

I encourage that we all win in our fantasies which looks like making up a happy ending when stepping out and taking a risk. When we feel excited it helps to say to ourselves, *I like this, I like feeling excited. I want more excitement in my life! This is fun.* This perspective will help you hold a positive focus and imagine a good outcome when things are unfolding other than you had planned.

Practice seeing the unknown as an exciting place of possibility for good things to occur. This kind of attitude shift moves us from upset to excitement.

Feeling **E**xcited **A**bout **R**eality and ready for what is next.

Oh No! to Oh Boy!

The future isn't here. We only have now. How we show up now influences later. If you see what might be good in your situation and focus on meeting that possibility you will be moved to engage by choosing to shift your focus to what might be, engaging in action to help it come about.

ঽ ৶ ৶ ৶ ঽ ৶

RX: Do This — Good Things Happening
Here and Now

- Win in your fantasies. How is what you have a gift not yet recognized? (Friends who care, margaritas while waiting in line, a 2-week vacation in warm, moist, sunshine ...)

- How might the future be even better as a result?

- Breathe into this possibility.

- The blessings already are. Claim the good things happening, *here and now.*

TIME TO PAUSE

Take a short timeout to do

Heart-Centered Breathing.

Slow your breathing down just a bit
while imagining inhaling and exhaling
through the middle of your chest.

Let each breath calm your
mind and emotions.

If you wish you can exhale with
a sighing sound.

Allow yourself to experience the peace
that is always present.

Ahhh … much better.

Take a next step, turn the page.

15. Designed for Failure

Success is going from failure to failure
without loss of enthusiasm.

Winston Churchill

꩜

Human beings are designed for failure. Perfection is impossible on this level. No matter how we attempt to manage our lives, something inevitably happens other than planned.

Imagine a mother tending to her two children. She is making her hungry five-year-old daughter a snack. Suddenly her 14-month old toddler falls and is now crying. Mom runs to pick up the little one. The older child is left to deal with her hunger. The mom, in a sense, has failed her.

You and I know she has not. Life happened and Mom is now dealing with a more immediate need, yet the hungry one is experiencing a failure in that moment.

Donald Winnicott's Good Enough Parenting theory beautifully demonstrates the gift of failure. The moment when the parent fails the child, the child is presented with the opportunity to move to the next level of maturation. The child in the above example has an opportunity to learn to soothe herself in this moment of loss. She is challenged to find a place of peace in the midst of chaos. This is an essential developmental task for all humans.

Learning how to calm down is one of the essential building blocks to health and well-being. When we can calm, we create an environment from which to learn and grow.

For those of you who have had children, or have ever watched a child learning to walk — or perhaps you were once a child — you are aware that walking comes with falling. As a parent you cannot do it for your child. The child needs to learn on her own. You may encourage, kneel down and open your arms and cheer her on as she's walking towards you. And if she falls (fails) she'll find her way to right herself, get up, and take another step.

Picking her up delays her opportunity to learn how to use her body, find balance, and develop her abilities and skills. Leaving her on the floor when she is clearly distressed and unable to calm down, or reprimanding her for falling, will also interfere with her natural progression and development. Good enough parenting is allowing the child to find their own way without rescuing them, while being there so they feel your presence.

It took me a while to change the interpretation I put on my life events, to realize that if life didn't go my way, the way I thought it was going to unfold, I wasn't being punished. No one was yelling at me for falling down while learning how to walk. And no one was picking me up and doing it for me either. I was in that space the child is in when she's learning how to walk.

I wasn't failing. Life wasn't withholding from me. Nobody had done me wrong. I was in that fertile ground of learning something new. As I learned to calm down, I was able to reinterpret my outer circumstances. I could see that whatever wasn't here yet, was an opportunity for me to learn how to step forward in a new way. At this point, my life changed radically.

Something will happen. Life is like that. It is designed that way in order to stimulate us to grow into next. Mastery in life is NOT in attempting to manage things so something doesn't happen — an impossible task. Mastery is about becoming competent in dealing with life on life's terms. When something happens, what do you do?

We can meet challenges kicking and screaming, or we can choose to learn with an open heart and mind, asking the question, "How is this a *for-me* experience?"

Recently, life happened in the life of a client that got in the way of her ability to work with me at a level of frequency she had been enjoying. She was upset as she found our sessions helpful. I asked her to wonder what the gift might be. It became apparent to her that she had grown to a place of readiness to let go of the training wheels.

At some point we do take the training wheels off the bike. Initially the experience is wobbly and uncertain, but in a brief amount of time we are riding down the street without the extra support.

Yes, we make mistakes. We act out of misunderstanding. This doesn't mean we are failures. It means we're in the process of learning what works.

The process of parenting and the seeming failures along the way are also those moments where a child needs to develop their own sense of self and learn how to calm down. How could any of that be seen as a failure?

We are designed to fail — ourselves and each other. If this is how it is supposed to be, how might you relate differently to your life when life happens? Are you willing to see that school in session? Perhaps you could trust that you have the capacity to learn and grow into *next*.

ᘖ ᘉ ᘖ

Hmmm — Ponder This:

What if you are not failing, but learning?

ᘖ ᘖ ᘉ

16. Eek Oh Boy! Leaving the Zone of the Known

I am always doing things I can't do — that's how I get to do them.

Pablo Picasso

༄༅

Life isn't necessarily a comfortable process (duh, Leslie!). Sometimes what gets in the way of *living by design* are the habits we have developed. This is commonly called the *comfort zone* or the *zone of the known.*

Imagine the comfort zone as a circle. Inside that circle are those things we are comfortable doing. Outside is everything else.

Consider what happens when you get to the edge of the comfort zone. Might it be by definition *uncomfortable?* You betcha. Uncomfortable can show up as fear, anxiety, anger, frustration, resignation, resentment, etcetera. What I call the Hamster Wheel of Hades delights. All leading to the question, why bother taking the risk? Might as well stay with what is familiar.

Problem is, the world is knocking at your door. Change has shown up inviting you out to play, or you've asked change to come over.

What do I mean by that?

Life happens. It is a dance. Sometimes Life drops changes in circumstances upon us. Like the Wicked Witch of the East. Where did that house come from? Drat. Now I'm dead.

Perhaps it looks like losing our job or even getting promoted. Our best friend moves. There is an accident. That sort of thing. Other times we are the instigator of change: we get married, have a child or two, go overseas on a holiday, go back to school, follow the Yellow Brick Road and invite some interesting characters to join us along the way.

Change moves us out of our comfort zone. Leaving the zone of the familiar puts us on alert. EEK! OH NO — something bad may happen. Fear arises and diminishes our willingness to risk venturing out of the zone of the known, thus diminishing our capacity for action. Unless the action is to flee back to the familiar, as the Cowardly Lion did when first meeting Oz, the Great and Terrible.

The good news is we can do something next. We can change Oh No! to Oh Boy! We do that by changing our focus. We remind ourselves it is just the Man Behind the Curtain messin' with us. Now that he is found out, it seems a balloon ride home is in our future.

Oh no, drat! Life happened again. Toto blew the trip home. Hmmm, maybe not. Perhaps something even better than a hot air balloon trip back to Kansas is coming to us now. Oh look, there she is! Glinda! I wonder what she has up those puffy sleeves of hers?

When I was 16, my then boyfriend was nuts about Tolkien's *The Hobbit* and the trilogy. As my self-appointed job was to be the best girlfriend, I too read the books. I fell in love with

Bilbo. Little did I know he was a symbol for the experience I was about to embark upon: The Reluctant Hero.

What does it mean to be a hero? Christopher Reeve described it as an ordinary individual who finds the strength to persevere and endure in spite of overwhelming obstacles.

To me it means rising to the challenge to do what is necessary to change the day. I meant to write *save the day,* but *change* is even better. If I don't show up and take action, I may not want to live in the results that are about to occur. Therefore, I choose to participate in a way that will make a positive difference.

There are many times I have not wanted to take action. Wanting and choosing are very different. If I wait until I want to participate, it may not happen. Especially if I don't feel like it. Many of us are like Bilbo sitting in his hobbit-hole, pipe in hand, sweets nearby, cozy in front of the warm fire. We do not want to go on an adventure, meet adversity or overcome challenges to serve the greater good. Who knows what might happen if we venture out? Let someone else do it.

Dorothy, famous for ruby slippers, the Yellow Brick Road and Oz, is also a reluctant hero. Lions and tigers and bears, oh my! Angry witches and flying monkeys and that giant head with fire belching out with every rise of the voice! Yet she overcame the Wicked Witch of the West. She chose to stand up to save her friend the Scarecrow. She confronted the dreadful green-faced witch, who melted into nothingness. That which had previously been terrifying disappeared.

We are bigger than whatever we are afraid of. The courage of our hearts will surpass any obstacle, especially when done sourced from love. Courage comes from the word *cœur* which means *heart* in French. So, the word courage means *of the heart,* or *from the heart.* Love is where courage emanates from, from the heart.

Like Bilbo, I wanted to stay home. I didn't want to go out into the imagined scary world filled with enemies and dark shadows that were going to get me. But I went anyway because no one else was going to make my life better. No one else was going to come rescue me, save me, pick me up and do it for me. Oh, fiddlesticks! It was up to me.

No, let me change that to, Yay! I was *forced* to do it for me. Not accurate — I *chose* it and still do. We *choose* to take action. That is the only way we transform our lives and make our world better.

I'm still reluctant at times. So what? Just because I don't feel like it or don't want to, doesn't mean I won't. I will. When we are willing, we learn how to do what needs to be done. Willingness leads to ability.

You may ask, *How does that happen?*

Well, willingness leads to action > leads to results > leads to learning > leads to new action > which leads to creative results > and new learning > which leads to new choices > and new actions > > > and so on.

Though Bilbo didn't want to, he was willing. As a reluctant hobbit, he chose to leave his hobbit-hole and the Shire and go out on a grand adventure, thus changing his life and the lives of everyone in Middle-Earth.

Problems are a gift. They take us out of our comfort zone. Every time we overcome a problem and create a solution we grow. We develop wisdom from the experience. Our abilities

develop. We become stronger, more able to meet the next chal-
lenge.

What about you? Are you willing to accept your reluctance
and take action anyway? Are you willing to step out of your
comfort to do what is next — even though you don't want to?

And if you are not willing, are you willing to be willing?

ॐ ℘ ৶ ৬ ॐ ℘

RX: Do This — One Itty-Bitty Baby Step at a Time

Moving past our comfort zone happens one step
at a time. That is all it takes, just the next step,
and then the next. Keep putting one foot in front
of the other. That is all that is required.

- Write down something you are wanting to
  grow into.

- Now, write down ONE itty-bitty action you
  could take, within the *next 24 hours* that will
  move you in that direction. (Just one itty-
  bitty teeny-weeny baby step action. Imagine
  this, in a year you could take 365 actions.
  Consider the progress you will make!)

- Now, take that action in the next 24 hours.
  Twenty-four hours is made up of 1,440
  minutes. Easy.

- Repeat until goal is attained.

- TA DA!

17. You Will be Tested

Thought creates our world and then says, 'I didn't do it'.

David Bohm

༄༅

Life, in the form of people, circumstances and situations, is constantly presenting us with opportunities to expand and lift. Life provides the chance to grow past a previous limitation into something *next.*

So, this is the deal — we are more than human beings. We are also human becomings. We are designed to evolve into something *next.* Growing is our thing. We like it. We have an inherent urge to stretch, try new things, explore and grow. Curious minds want to explore and experiment. That's the fun part of having a human brain.

As human becomings, there is always *next.* We are constantly evolving. Life is designed to nudge us forward. We continue to stretch the boundaries of our comfort zone and we grow. Our zone of the familiar has now expanded and we are now ready for the next adventure.

The game of creating a life you love, stretching past what was familiar, provokes thinking designed to keep you from becoming the next best version of yourself. As you set off on your adventure of creation, everything that has kept you from having what you want will poke its head up to challenge your commitment.

This is good news. Good news because part of waking up to who you really are and what you have to give, is discovering how you have, up until now, held yourself back. Now you can do something different, expand into new possibilities. That means making room for a bigger version of you.

Except for one thing — the Mind Monsters don't want you to grow. Better safe than risk failure or something worse! They begin to crawl out from under the bed telling you to stay tucked in. No need to go out to do what it takes. You'll never make it happen. It's too much! They want you to stay the same, quaking in bed with the covers over your head. Boo!

What are these Mind Monsters you may ask? They are those pesky thoughts that seem to rear up bigger than life, taunting you to stay put and not grow into *next*. You can hear them in your head yelling, *oh no! Oh, no! The sky is falling.* They tell you what you should or shouldn't do. They imagine the future and tell you that you can't handle it. They look into the past and fill you with regret and woe. They don't want you to step out of your comfort zone. Don't go! Don't go, they yell. Stay put and let me torture you with confusion and doubt.

Do you remember those Western movies where the outlaws made some young kid dance by shooting bullets at his feet? That's the kinda gang this is. They make you dance as in jumping up and down out of fear.

Let me tell you a secret. Their words are lies, designed to trick you into submission. Lock you in the prison of your mind. Festering with their stinking thinking. PeeEwww.

Let me introduce you to a few of the most obvious ones. The leader of the pack is The Should Monster! Following close behind is the:

> The Doubt Monster
>
> The Worry Monster
>
> The Not Good Enough Monster
>
> The How Dare You Monster
>
> The What Will They Think Monster
>
> The I Don't Matter Monster
>
> The Shame Monster
>
> The What If Monster ... and so on

Don't be frightened. There are more. They are part of the Misery Making Mechanism of the Mind. They thrive on mischief by speaking words of judgment, discouragement and limitation so that you stay in the zone of the familiar and not upset the status quo. Those Monsters love to distract us from the reality that we are on purpose in the direction we want to go. They feed off creativity that can be invested elsewhere.

No need to judge the Monsters. They were useful when we were living in small tribes. At that time, it was essential for us to be able to count on one another in particular ways, so as a group, we could survive. Creativity was more a risk than an asset. Staying the same, doing the familiar, that which worked, led to living another day.

But that was then and this is now. As you are reading this, you have clearly had enough of being defined, confined, restrained and contained. You are ready to Lift Up into the unknown, engaging in the process of creating something even better than what already is.

Mind abuse is a result of listening to the Mind Monsters. Allow them to dominate your thinking and they become more powerful and nastier. If you don't feed the Monsters, who feast on your attention, they starve and go away. You must be tenacious in your commitment to ignore them, for when hungry for your attention they *can* get really ugly.

You can't stop the Mind Monsters from talking. You can change the station, directing your thinking elsewhere.

One of my clients declared at the session right after I introduced him to the Mind Monsters, "My brain is trying to kill me!" After I stopped laughing, he added, "But I'm onto them now! I noticed this week by not listening to what they are saying I am freer and more creative."

As far as I can tell their mischief serves a higher purpose. They are challenging you to see if you are willing to be who you truly are, rather than buying into the setup that you are a victim of circumstances.

I invite you to watch a priceless Sesame Street video based on the popular children's book, *"The Monster at the End of This Book – starring Lovable Grover,"* (It's worth searching for the video on YouTube.) It beautifully represents how we scare ourselves with our thinking. Watch Grover as he invests in thinking that what will appear at the end of the book is more than he can handle.

It isn't true for him. It isn't true for you either.

NOW A STORY

I was preparing to drive to a venue about 90 minutes from my home to facilitate an event on a cold Monday in early January. The phone rang. It was Mary wanting to know if I was coming. I wondered why the call. Of course, I was coming. The event was full to capacity. It's not like me to be a no show.

She continued, letting me know a blizzard was on the way.

I told Mary I would be there no matter what. She invited me to stay at her home if the storm left me unable to drive home. I thanked her and got off the phone.

I revised my plan taking into consideration the new weather forecast. I began packing an overnight bag, planning to leave my house as soon as possible. Intention: getting to the venue ahead of the storm.

While I was preparing, my brain was full of noise. Voices warring with each other to get my attention. Complaints about the change in circumstances. Worrying about getting stuck in a blizzard. Fretting no one will come out in the storm. Lamentations about poor me, why did this have to happen to me, and so on. The Monsters were out, salivating.

I was caught up in Crazy Brain and feeling stress in my body, pushing myself to get out the door. Suddenly I heard a voice. It was *not* a Monster voice. It said, with loving firmness, "Shut up and show up!"

That got my attention.

I began to laugh.

What's with all the noise? Based on my actions, I was clearly going to the event no matter what the Monsters thought about it.

With the self-amusement came a quieting. The Monsters must have been thwarted by wisdom. It didn't matter what I *thought*, it mattered what I *did.*

End of story: Only three of the people registered didn't come. Two were because of illness and the third had car trouble. The storm was not an issue for any of them. By the time the event had ended, the storm had ended too. The roads were clear. I easily made it home.

It doesn't matter what we think, it matters what we do.

ᘒ ᔿ ᘔ ᘓ ᘒ ᔿ

RX: Do This — You Are Bigger Than the Monsters

- Which Monster stops you the most?

- Notice when you don't show up for yourself or for other people, because you're investing in the stories the Monsters are telling you. (Remember the voice, *Shut up and show up.*)

- Now that you know it's just friendly, Lovable Grover, what will you do differently when the noise begins in your head?

18. Willingness

Willingness opens the door to all life's possibilities.

Byron Katie

༄

Would you like a tool that quells the Monsters and has them scurrying back into the shadows of nothingness from which they came? No? Yes?

I knew you'd say Yes.

The Power Tool that you already possess is your willingness. Willingness opens us to learning. Willingness allows us to move towards possibility. Willingness makes room for guidance and support.

What is it to be willing? It is being inclined to do something; the act of choosing; the power of choice; volitional.

Scared or excited, it doesn't matter. What matters is that you are willing. Remember Bilbo, reluctant but willing. He chose to participate.

Once you become willing, your dream, your goal, your commitment will pull you forward. Your willingness will guide you into action that will take you where you want to go.

You don't have to know how to make what you want happen. All that is required is that you are willing. The willingness sets you up for learning. It moves you into action. It guides your discovery of *how.*

Notice what you experience when you declare, *I am willing to do whatever it takes to bring my goal (dream, commitment), into reality.* You may observe a tangible physical response. Fluttery, queasy, butterflies stirring in the belly come with the territory.

When we get to the edge of our comfort zone and step out, we are, by definition, going to be uncomfortable. The Monsters stick their heads out from under the bed. You could recognize the discomfort as feedback that you are on course. On course in moving toward your intended destination.

During the process of writing this book, I took myself on a 5-day solitary retreat so I could be fully engaged in the writing process. One afternoon, the Monsters began to speak. "Boring!" one exclaimed. Another chimed in, "Do you really think anyone cares about this?" and so on. It wasn't pretty or encouraging.

At first, I was taken aback. The voices had momentarily destabilized me. Then I righted myself, realizing that no matter what they said I was going to finish the book. I was willing. I was in action. I was determined. As I moved into the clarity of my commitment, the voices went silent.

If we want what we want, we must become willing to do, to be and to have whatever it takes. Including the willingness to be uncomfortable. To not know. To make mistakes. To keep taking action as we travel towards our goal. Remember that the first step is to be willing. Willingness will bring the ability.

Are you willing to do what it takes to become the person you yearn to be, the person who is living a life of your own design? Are you willing to own your life as a creative work in process, and yourself as the artist calling it into reality? Are you willing to commit to live by design rather than by default?

Are you willing? If yes, then even if you are reluctant, afraid, and uncomfortable while the Mind Monsters are screaming in your head — keep going.

19. A White Dot Waiting to Happen

For fast acting relief, try slowing down.

Lily Tomlin

ঞ৶

What is it that just crawled over my arm? Ewww, it's a giant black ant! I look down and I see another. I turn my chair and there are two more. Carpenter ants crawling all over the floor of my office.

Quickly I place a call to Jim who is my designated pest control guy. As service is his middle name, he shows up first thing the next morning. Thank you, Jim.

The treatment works best if I move the furniture away from the wall. I wiggle the cabinet where my files are stored away from the wall and take a peek. The dust and debris that had accumulated was kinda, well, ick.

Now, you know if the ants hadn't appeared, and Jim hadn't been there to take care of business, there would have been no dirt to be cleared away. I wouldn't have known it was there. So, it makes sense that Jim (or the ants) were to blame for me finding myself engaged in some deeper cleaning than I had planned on doing that day (or any day soon). If only the ants had left me alone, all would be well. If I don't know about it, well, it doesn't exist.

But nooooo, there were ants. Jim did appear. I moved the furniture and discovered what had been hidden. You and I know it wasn't Jim (or the ants) who were responsible for the clean-up. Their appearance just made me aware of cleaning that was available to be done.

Yet, when something happens in our life and we find ourselves upset, we tend to blame Jim (or the ants) or whatever or whoever it was that showed us where the debris was hidden. Instead of thanking the outer for an opportunity to clean up the inner, many of us wail ... *I'm upset and it is YOUR FAULT!*

The fact was the dirt was there and now there was disturbance. (Or dust-urbance in this case.) Who would you say is causing the distress?

In my book, *Life Happens: What Are YOU Going to Do About It?,* I talk about the perturbing finger. Do you remember that chapter? Who made the dot? Who is upsetting me? The dust? The ants? Jim's request for me to move my furniture from the wall?

Allow me to recap. Let's pretend you and I are in the same room physically. Now imagine me asking your permission to touch your forearm and you saying yes. I reach out and gently press my finger onto your arm and ask you what you notice. You look at your arm as I pull my hand away and say, "Leslie, there is a spot on my arm where your finger was."

It is true. I have touched your arm gently and as I take my hand away, we both see a white dot appear where my finger was.

I now ask you, "Who did that?"

If you are like most people, you will reply, "You did that, Leslie. You made the spot."

Hmmm, but what if I reach out and touch the arm of the chair you are sitting on? Perhaps the top of your shoe? What happens?

Nothing at all.

The pigment of the chair cloth and your shoe remains as it was.

So, I ask you again, who made the temporary mark on your arm? Who made the white dot?

The finger is just the external influence that provoked your body's reaction to the perturbance.

Conclusion: You are a White Dot waiting to happen.

Oy boy!

Yet, don't we go through life declaring, *I'm a White Dot and it is YOUR fault?* I'm upset and it is your fault because your finger showed me where the place is in me that is an upset waiting to happen.

Just like the dust behind the cabinet. It was there before I moved the furniture. It was there before Jim arrived. It was there before the ants jumped out of the tree onto the roof of my house and crawled their way onto my arm. (Ewww.)

A client told me after he had started reading my book, "I had to put the book down after Chapter 6. That White Dot blew my mind. I couldn't think straight for two weeks. I'm afraid to keep reading. What else do you have in there?"

This is a big deal.

You are a White Dot waiting to happen.

Who is to blame for this fix I'm in?

This is good news. *If* you are a White Dot waiting to happen and someone inadvertently banged into you and now you're upset, you get to heal that. You didn't even know there was a

White Dot there until it revealed itself. I didn't know there was so much dust behind the cabinet until I pulled it away from the wall.

I could choose to be grateful for the clean-up opportunity, as could you. You could say to the perturbing finger, "Thank you for showing me where my next area of personal growth work is located, because I don't want to live in reaction to my life. Life happens and I'm so easily upset."

Ahhh, an opportunity to calm. Conscious Awareness Lifting Me up. Using the White Dot as an occasion to lift from reactivity into creativity.

What if *pow*, life happens, leading to *ow*, is the doorway to *wow*? Wow, I didn't know there was a mess behind the cabinet, I didn't realize I was a White Dot waiting to happen. Pow, Ow, Wow. Thank you for showing that to me.

What if White Dots are blessings in disguise and once activated call our loving attention into action? I now have the opportunity to show up and participate in greater self-love, which right now looks like getting the broom and the trash bin and getting to work.

NOW A STORY

A client came in one day eager to report a win. He was learning how he was a White Dot waiting to happen. He was also learning about the power of calm. He had an experience that woke him up to how a peaceful presence can serve the ending of White Dot distress. This is what he told me:

It was a hot day. I was crawling down Roosevelt Road, in heavy traffic. We were stopped, but I had left space to allow someone to turn left onto the side street

Lo and behold, a giant Hummer comes up on the inside lane, passing everyone waiting in traffic and wedged into the space I had made for left turners.

I went ballistic. I MF'd the guy. I called him every name in the book. I was lit.

I pulled up next to him at the next light. I rolled down my window and yelled, "Why do you think you get to go before everyone else? That was a blanketyblank move!"

He calmly turned to me and asked, "Why does it bother you so much?"

I replied by calling him a name.

With complete calm he asked again, "What I did isn't that big a deal. Why does it bother YOU so much?"

His calm made me wonder what I was really angry about. It had nothing to do with him. It was other things.

When I realized it, I said to him, "You are right. Peace and love baby, see ya'," and I drove away.

Yay to Mr. Hummer, staying calm in the midst of an attack. Yay to my client who owned his White Dot. That's all we can do. We are White Dots waiting to happen. Thank you for showing me what is really bothering me. Now I can do something about it.

ॳ ℘ ॐ ॺ ॺ ℘

RX: Do This — White Dot to Wide Open Wonder = WOW

What gets us stuck is thinking we know, thinking we're right, blaming ourselves or someone else, versus wondering, being curious. Wonder shifts us to a place which opens us to possibilities.

Let's experiment with the appearance of the White Dot. Let's say this isn't a problem. Suppose it's a creative opportunity. An opportunity for healing.

- While considering what the opportunity might be, take that blame finger that is pointing at that person, situation, circumstance, or yourself for upsetting you, and turn it around. Now, place it on either your chin, heart, cheek or temple with an audible, *Hmmm ...*

- Say the *Hmmm ...* aloud as it integrates both sides of brain. Start the sentence before you think about it and let the mind fill in the blank.

  Hmmm ... maybe this is showing me ___.

  Hmmm ... perhaps this is revealing that ___.

  Hmmm ... it might be that I could learn ___.

- *Hmmm ...*

Keep wondering and shifting up until you realize there is no problem to solve. In fact, you have been given a gift, a chance to grow into something *next.*

Life is happening *for* you, not *to* you.

20. The 'F' Word

The weak can never forgive. Forgiveness
is the attribute of the strong.

Mahatma Ghandi

ॐ

A client and I were exploring her resistance to giving up her resentments. I suggested forgiveness as the doorway to freedom, to which she replied, "Oh, the 'F' word!" We both cracked up. When we quieted, I related a story of a friend who told me his marriage ended in divorce. He said she refused to forgive him. There was no big breach, just the normal misunderstandings that occur in the course of a marriage and she refused to 'F' him.

My client burst out laughing and so did I as we both know unFORGIVEness is a process of withholding. The woman probably refused to 'F' him in other ways as well. Wait a minute, let's be clear ... I mean F as in FAVOR him, as in being generous and kind.

We decided that the session would be a version of Sesame Street and today we would be devoted to all F words related to forgiveness or the lack thereof. Why not? Reason wasn't supporting her in shifting off her position, thus setting her FREE. Yes, FREEdom is an F word and is directly related to FOR-

GIVENESS. Forgiveness is a gesture FOR ourselves. In choosing to FORGIVE we set ourselves FREE. It has nothing to do with the other person.

When we are unFORgiving, we tend to FILTER reality with a sorting mechanism that looks for how the other person is FAILING us, therefore, generating evidence as to how we are right that it is their FAULT we're upset.

One of the truths about human existence is that we have control over very little, especially other people. We cannot FIX anything. The FAILED attempts to FIX keeps us in the illusion that we are victims, victims to something outside our control. My client recognized this. She saw there is a part of her that is comfortable in victim mode, that her resentment is juicy to her. 'Her' as in her ego.

Yup, it is juicy to the ego. The ego loves to be right, to control and to blame. It makes meaning and identity by weaving the fabric of life to suit the story it is attached to. This juice is really poison for it makes us sick and tired, stuck in a very unpleasant story about our lives. And the ego does this with FERVOR, FALSE enthusiasm, FIGHTING to be right about being wronged! It is a FACTORY of FALSEHOOD that keeps us FORLORN.

Whew, we were on a roll. She took the baton by telling me she FABRICATES FANTASY that FREAKS her out and that it is a FOLLY to do the same thing over and over expecting a different result. Meaning that no matter how much she settles into unFORgiveness, her husband, or whoever, never seems to get that she has unmet needs she wants addressed. All he seems to do is run in the other direction. No wonder she feels a bit FRUSTRATED.

She saw how doing the same thing over and over, only louder and more often, did not get her what she wanted. This had her realize she could come up with other ways to re*solve* her problems. She saw there might actually be another right answer if she was willing to FORMULATE other possibilities.

She realized she had been FORBIDDING herself to be happy by not participating in the process of FORGIVENESS, which could lead to greater ease and joy in life. UnFORgivness is like that. We hurt ourselves in an attempt to hurt other people.

With a big smile on her face, she told me she was a FAKE and has been living in a FACADE, putting on a FRONT by telling herself a FLAWED story and convincing herself it was *the truth*. Instead, she saw the illusion, the FRAUDULENCE of right/wrong/good/bad, which is FALSE. There is no such reality. Life just is. We are asked to meet the moment with FORTITUDE.

That was her word — FORTITUDE — which means courage. As I have mentioned, courage comes from the French word *cœur* meaning *heart*. We all know forgiveness is an action of the heart. It takes great courage to choose a path of Loving.

I suggested she could FABRICATE FANTASIES that support her in FLOURISHING, by realizing FORGIVENESS is the FUEL that opens the heart and restores us to peace.

We laughed so much enjoying our FUN, that we decided we'd take on the Ws next time. Perhaps we will turn WORRY into WONDER!

How about you? Are you WEARY of WITHHOLDING Loving from yourself and others? Perhaps it is time to do something different. Maybe you could try on FORGIVEness.

If you don't like it, you could close yourself back up, cross your arms and legs, put on a pout and see if anyone comes running to save you from your choice. Someone might, though I haven't seen it happen yet. You could take the risk to see if you're the first. Or you could choose to FOR GIVE.

Be FOR GIVING yourself a break!

I have experienced in my life, and have witnessed in the lives of many others, that FORGIVENESS is one of the most powerful POWER MOVES we have been given to navigate the circumstances of an unpredictable life.

21. Oh Right, Forgiveness

Failure is a judgment. This is very simple.
If there is no judgment, there is no failure.

John Morton

ॐ

There is a calm that comes from knowing I have a choice. This is where I am powerful, in the domain of choices and actions. If I don't like the experience I am having, I can DO something about it. Even if there are no actions to take in the world, I can change my attitude about what is going on. I have choice.

Choices are empowering. Power as in the ability to participate in life and harvest the outcomes of our actions. It is a blessing to be aware that I have options. This is true freedom. The freedom of choice.

The freedom to choose is the essence of responsibility. The ability to respond versus merely to react. Responsibility is the Doorway to Heaven, lifting us off the Hamster Wheel of Hades into the world of invention, creativity and resilience.

We are more than reactive animals. We have choice. We can choose to lift into our higher nature, to access the gift that is our greater selves. This is the joy of living and has nothing to do with our outer circumstances. It is an inner process of personal freedom through choice.

As you can see in the previous chapter, forgiveness is a choice. It doesn't just automatically happen. Even if someone apologizes, if you don't choose to forgive, you are still stuck in unforgiveness. Unforgiveness is an offspring of the Should Monster married to the How Dare You Monster.

We forgive as an antidote to judgments. We aren't forgiving actions or behavior. Life is neutral. Our circumstances are impersonal. The personal part is how we participate. How we choose to relate to the situation.

The way we interpret an occurrence is the experience we get to live in. How else can we account for the fact that someone experiences joy in a similar situation that causes someone else to fall into depression?

When it snows, some folks get cold, other people go skiing. Those who get cold are interpreting the weather one way. Those who bundle up and jump in the car to go play, another. Same outer circumstance, different response.

Imagine judging the weather for messing up your plans. You were intending to take a long walk and soak up some sun. The snow triggered one of your White Dots. Just like publishing my first book triggered one of mine.

NOW A STORY

I was driving to Chicago on a beautiful sunny day with deep blue sky as a backdrop for the lush green of the summer. The world was expressing a deep and nourishing peace, yet I was disturbed. I was agitated. My belly was whirling. My jaw was tight. My breath high in my chest.

It was right after my first book was published. Stepping out of the familiar into the world of being a *published author* was a stretch. A sign of expansion and growth. As I was writing the book, I would hit pockets of agitation and anxiety. Sometimes I would stop writing, other times I persevered until I broke through.

Now the book was published. Both it and I had come out. My world had changed due to my actions and I was standing differently on planet Earth. On this particular day the agitation was making me nauseous. I was quite distracted by the sensation in my belly. The Mind Monsters were out from under the bed, as will happen when we move past the edges of what is familiar into new territory. They were making lots of noise about how silly I was to put myself out into the world as I had.

They were testing me. Will I hold steady in this place of expansion? Am I willing to claim this new space? Will I breathe myself open to even greater possibilities or will I let fear move me back into what was familiar, which I had deemed safe?

I had the awareness of how much of my life I used to spend in this upset place. Years of practice and study has shown me how to lift out of this disturbance into something peaceful and more powerful.

Once again, I noticed myself judging myself. The part in me that continues to believe that one day my shift will come, that I will lift up and never drift back into disturbance, was upset about my upset.

Here I am in distress, again! Clearly, I have not done my work for there is still work to do!

Silly me. The wisdom in me knows the human condition is a drift and shift experience. Thus, I continue to practice Calming Down and Lifting Up. Over the years I fall down less often, get up faster and stay up longer. Progress on planet Earth.

Even in the midst of agitation I experienced gratitude for the recognition that these moments were less frequent and of shorter duration. Meanwhile, I didn't want to stay here if I had a choice. I asked myself what to do?

I began to mentally skim through the pages of *Life Happens: What Are YOU Going to Do About It?*. I landed on the chapter called forgiveness. That felt right. Forgiveness.

Yes, the gift of forgiveness, the gift of freedom. I choose to be For Giving!

My approach to forgiveness is not about forgiving behavior or actions. It's about forgiving the judgments we placed against life. The judgment that life *should* be doing something other than it does, or that I should be behaving differently than I do (such as never, ever, ever getting upset again).

I reminded myself to stop pretending I know what I do not know. I began forgiving myself for judging myself. I spoke the words aloud. On and on the judgments arose like plates in the cafeteria line. As one judgment dissolved with the healing balm of self-forgiveness, another one appeared before me. I continued to use the power tool of forgiveness to send them back into the nothingness from which they came. Spiritual warrior in action.

Judgments are just thoughts. Thoughts are just peristalsis of the brain. Nothing substantial there.

After a while my mind went quiet. There was peace. My belly was calm, my breath deep and quiet.

A moment later I had totally forgotten what I had been upset about.

Waking up from the victim trance is not easy. Most of us were raised in a tribe that allows the Monsters to roam without supervision. If you are not subjecting yourself under your own tyranny, there are other people's Monsters ready to pounce. We have to really want to be free from the constraints of the mind and the stories we tell ourselves. Right, wrong, good, bad, rules and judgments keeping us imprisoned.

It is up to us to make the choices and take the actions to release ourselves. We must be willing to stop judging, to stop pretending we know what we do not know. When you relax into not knowing and allow yourself to just be, you give yourself a gift of calmness and of peace.

Yes, it takes effort, attention and diligence. But once awake to the choice to lift higher, choose joy, participate in creativity and loving, why would you ever want to go back to sleep? For me, awake, engaged and participating, even when it's hard, is much better than sleeping under a doormat hoping nobody will step on me.

I have trained myself to realize when I am agitated, whiney, withdrawn or irritable that there is something I can pay attention to within. I shift my attention to the disturbance and engage in calming down, expanding until I come back Home to peace.

Peace is our natural state. Just like the dog curled up in the sun, or romping around in the woods, curious about what might be discovered, we too are our best selves when sourcing from the calm center of our beingness.

The opportunity with *life happening* is to embrace it as a teacher; showing us how to do better. Forgiving ourselves for judging helps calm our Crazy Brain so we can embrace what is here for us.

Instead of withholding, which comes with unforgiveness, we can choose to be *for giving*. We can choose to be *for* the action of *giving* up our argument with reality and *for giving* ourselves and others a break from our Crazy Brain judgments. We thus are choosing to be *for giving* loving kindness to self and other.

22. Forget It!

Do not take life too seriously.
You will never get out of it alive.

Elbert Hubbard

༄༅

We don't have to be condemned by our past. We free our-
selves by not only forgiving but by forgetting as well. We forgive
the judgments we hold against ourselves or other people re-
garding behavior and circumstances that we find upsetting.
Upsetting in that they didn't go the way they *should* have. That
should word again.

(By now you know I consider *should* a 'bad word'. I would
love it if, when you notice it running around in your mind or
coming out of your mouth that you hear me lovingly tell you to
go wash out your mouth and come back with a mouth full of
coulds.)

Once we truly forgive, which means we notice an upward
shift of energy, our heart is open, and there is an inner peace.
Now it is time to forget. We don't forget the learning we gained
from the experience. We take that with us. Wisdom comes from
making sense of our mistakes, hurts, and disturbances.

What we forget is the hurt, the disturbance, our opinion
about what occurred. We stop dragging the past along every-
where we go.

How can you forget? I learned a way that is very powerful, so put on your seat belts and here we go ...

RX: Do This — Forget It!

- Bring to mind a person, situation or circumstance that has your hackles up. You may be the person with whom you are upset.
- Do your forgiveness work until you have freed yourself.
- Next, fill yourself up with your own loving kindness ... remember, forgiving is about being FOR the action of GIVING ... and what we give is loving kindness.
- Fill yourself up until you are overflowing and then extend your loving to the other person (especially if you don't want to).
- Imagine your loving as white light and fill the person, situation or circumstance with that light until the disturbance disappears. Voila. The negativity exists no more. You dissolved whatever it was, hmmm, I seem to have forgotten, into nothingness.
- Take a breath and notice the expansive feeling of freedom.
- Ahhh, much better.

If for some reason, that pesky mind decides to recreate the disturbance, go through the whole process again. Repetition will create new neural pathways that are habituated to sending loving kindness to disturbance.

How cool is that?

৵৯ ৵ঢ় ৵৯

Hmmm — Ponder This:

What if *life happens* and we choose to welcome it?

Thank you *for giving* me this experience.

৵৯ ৵৯ ৵ঢ়

23. Another Way to Lift: Giving a BOB.

Wonder, rather than doubt, is the root of all knowledge.

Abraham Joshua Heschel

༄༅

Raise your hand if you have ever been upset because someone or something didn't show up in your life according to your expectations. Is it just me or is this a part of the human experience we are all having?

Okay, I can see you. You can put your hand down now.

A few years back I ran into BOB. He helps me choose kindness towards myself and others whenever something happens that disturbs my mind and triggers the grumps. BOB stands for choosing to give the Benefit Of the Benefit.

BOB for short. Generous BOB giving double dividends — a benefit AND another benefit!

Let's say something happens I wasn't expecting or wanting. As we've been exploring, it is like us humans to get upset when something goes amiss when we are expecting smooth sailing. It's a survival strategy to come present to what is and make a choice based on new circumstances. It IS upsetting. Appropriately so. Life continues to disturb us, calling us to come present to our new circumstances. We need to pay special attention — now — in order to navigate the situation.

The difficulty is with the mind. The mind loves to tell a story about everything. When things go awry it tends to judge and complain, rather than doing what it is very good at: observe, collect data and strategize.

Upset is just fine. Upset moves us to a next step, which is what we want: to move in the direction we'd prefer to go. The problem is getting stuck in disturbance and falling into the grumps. The grumps don't do it for us. The grumps keep us focused on what isn't, rather than call us present to what is. Remember the experiment with the color red (Chapter 14: Feeling Excited about Reality)? The red is in the room (possibility for creative action) but the grumps are filtering the mind so that what is seen is what is wrong.

This is where BOB comes in. We give the benefit of the benefit, meaning we assume nothing was done on purpose to hurt or harm us in any way. Stuff just happens. Life is like that. We extend the benefit of this assumption into our world and receive the benefit of this blessing upon ourselves in the form of calming the upset. Now we can access our inner resources to make choices and take action based on what is here, now.

BOB helps us change how we relate to the situation. If we change the way we habitually interpret the experiences of our lives, we will *change* our lives. I'm not kidding.

A few of my clients and friends have made BOB their new best friend. One client told me when she notices she is in disturbance, especially when she is irritated with her husband, she realizes she left BOB at home. She takes a moment, a calming breath, and retrieves him. That is a wise woman.

Upset is a wake-up call to notice what thoughts are being invested in. If you are ruminating on who is to blame for the fix you are in, or judging whatever is going on as wrong or bad, you have probably met the anti-BOB.

Anti-BOB is a bully. He is *not* your friend. He is mean, bossy, never satisfied and a grouch. He will make you miserable. He already has. He is the one who runs the *Life Sucks and then You Die* movie on the screen of your mind, yucking it up in the projection booth while you are having a melt down because the movie isn't going the way you think it *should*. The anti-BOB is one of the Should Monsters.

You could use this disturbance as a Power Move moment. You could see *upset* as a flash warning on the dashboard of your car, indicating you are close to trouble. An indicator that it is time to take a corrective action. It seems you've left home without BOB and the anti-BOB is having his way with you. Turn the car around and go fetch good-hearted, give the Benefit Of the Benefit, BOB.

Stop the car. Take a few deep breaths. Turn your attention to the source of the upsetting movie. Notice it's just anti-BOB up to his silly tricks again. Reach up into the booth like the super-hero you are and flick him away. Or if you prefer, you can exhale him away.

Now go Home by putting your hand on your heart and taking a deep breath (or however you and BOB have worked out getting together). Invite BOB back into your car and off you go with BOB as your companion, meeting whatever occurs with beneficence.

Much better, yes?

NOW A STORY

I use this tool quite a bit. I had posted an invitation to a workshop and a book signing event at a local bookstore. Someone I know who lives near town posted in the comment box that she'd love to go but needed a ride. She asked me to take her.

The request for a ride was irritating at first. When I present, I choose to get to the venue early. I stay after the event as long as there are folks who want to speak with me. I wasn't sure how to manage driving this woman while taking care of myself as well. At the same time, I appreciated her desire to join us and was willing to find a way to be of service.

I noticed Crazy Brain going on-and-on about the imposition. I chose to look for another way to see the situation. Then I got it. Perhaps she was doing a social media move of *liking*. Commenting as a way to support me.

Giving her a BOB quieted me. I wrote her a kindhearted text to explore how we could get her to the venue. I quickly received a reply. She couldn't come because she was working. It turns out she *was* just offering support!

Even if that was not the case, my willingness to see the situation beyond my initial irritation put me in a gracious place. I was now able to sincerely reach out to her with kindness.

That's how it works. Annoyances, little irritations, minor stressors can be managed with grace when we choose to see them through different eyes.

Oh, there is more! BOB has morphed into something *next*. Just like us, he continues to go from *good* to *better than that*. BOB has learned he can transform himself from a benefit into a blessing and extend his goodness out into the world.

If you are like me, you are wondering *how the hey does he do that?* Well, he discovered when he calms himself and shifts to peace, he is able to look for the blessing in the moment.

Way to go SuperHero BOB ... the **BENEFIT OF THE BLESSING!**

’ ’ ’ ’ ’ ’

RX: Do This — Put On Your Blessing Seeking Glasses

Many of us tend to struggle with embracing the process of life and the changes that accompany living. Life happens and it is a problem. Rather than thwarting you, what if life was actually serving you? Might you be willing to interpret life happening as a blessing in disguise?

- Get in the habit of asking better questions. Notice what is different when you shift your focus with an empowered question.

- Put your blessing-seeking glasses on and ask: *Hmmm, if BOB were here, what would he tell me was the good in this experience?*

ॐ ॐ ॐ

Hmmm — Ponder This:

Where would BOB say the blessings are
in your life right now?

ॐ ॐ ॐ

24. And the Frog Jumps

Do it badly; do it slowly; do it fearfully;
do it any way you have to but do it.

Steve Chandler

ॐ

Imagine this. There is a giant-sized bull frog sitting on a lily pad in the middle of a pond. He decides to jump off. How many frogs remain on that lily pad?

Just one. The same giant-sized bull frog that was serenading you with his deep croak just moments before. He decided to jump off. Deciding is not jumping. Making a decision is not doing the deed. Not the same thing at all.

As a matter of fact, making a decision without taking action puts us on the thinking-about-doing and not on the doing train. Thinking about doing — *hmmm, when might I do this?* — *I really don't want to do this* — *what if it doesn't turn out as I hope?* — *it could be really dreadful* — *and so on.* Thinking without action, on the rails to nowhere.

Best course of action: once a decision is made — actually do it. Action produces results which can be evaluated and lead to new action. Frog jumps off lily pad in pursuit of that fly. Frog misses. Frog gets to jump again. Eventually frog gets belly full of flies. Yum.

The frog who doesn't jump, also doesn't eat. Not eating leads to thinking about food. Thinking about food isn't eating food. Eating flies is what is required.

Don't avoid the relationship with what is in front of you. Once you make a decision, take that decision into action. You do not have to fully understand before you take action. Understanding happens through participation.

There was a time when I had a bout of poison ivy. It was dreadful. Beyond description horrible. It turned out to be a gift because I realized no matter how many words, gestures or sounds I used I couldn't get anyone to understand how awful the experience was. The experience was the teacher. Not until you sit on a tack, stub your toe, or miss your exit because you were daydreaming, do you understand the experience of sitting on a tack, stubbing your toe or missing your exit, or how awful poison ivy is.

At some point it is time to turn thinking about doing into jumping into the experience. Decide and then do it. Full-out participation. Thought is not required, only action. This is where life and learning occur. Not in the head. In the doing. Action turns thinking into real experience. Action moves you out of your head and into your life.

I have come to realize that sitting on the lily pad thinking about what is in front of me to do, and not involving myself in the doing, is agitating. Agitation is upsetting. Thinking about thinking about thinking throws me on the Hamster Wheel of Hades, pretending I'm going someplace but remaining in the same spot. Distraction action. Active non-action.

NOW A STORY

Talking about jumping into the water ... have you ever stood at the edge of a pond, a lake, a swimming pool, thinking about jumping in? Imagining you were about to jump in? Wondering what it would feel like once you were in?

I was in Montana in the Bitterroots. We had hiked up to a lake named Gem due to the magnificent color of the water. The lake had been made by a glacier. It was so cold that fish couldn't live in it.

Two of us had the thought of jumping in. One of us did. That one wasn't me. I was the one on the edge of the rock cliff thinking about jumping in. Especially after my friend had plunged in and came to the surface with a blood-curdling yell.

At that point I was thinking about not jumping in. Yet she was still breathing, even laughing as she pulled herself out of the water.

I faced the reality that thinking about jumping wasn't going to get me in the water. Nothing to do but GOoooooooo!

There is nothing to do when there is something to do, but to do what there is to do.

25. Use Everything for Your Upliftment, Learning and Growth

The impediment to action advances action.
What stands in the way becomes the way.

Marcus Aurelius

꙰

True intelligence comes from making use of everything in our lives. What we're given. The raw material we use to create.

Arguing with the gift of our circumstances is stupid. Stupid is stuck. Stupid is investing energy going nowhere. I've been told karma is spelled S-T-U-P-I-D. Stupid equals no learning, no growth, no evolution.

Stupid is not ignorant. Ignorant means we don't know. Not knowing leads to learning. Stupid is refusing to learn. Therefore, karma is an opportunity for learning. That's it. Learn and grow or suffer.

Anytime we're pushing up against something, we can either see it as an adversary that's trying to thwart us, or a teacher challenging us to grow and develop. Like a snake shedding its skin so it can become something *next*. Or a chicken pressing against the shell it has been contained in, in order to get free. Or those shoes. Your favorite red shoes, now too tight in the toes. Drat. Time for a new pair of shoes.

Seemingly there is some sort of restriction that we are fighting against that isn't against us at all. It's actually there for us to grow the muscle that's needed so we can develop into our next level of evolutionary expression.

Arguing keeps us stuck in the tight, restrictive place of the familiar. Instead, we can relax at the edges, take a breath and expand into *next*.

Here are some questions to ponder:

- What if life happens to wake us up to our next opportunity for growth and learning? What if upsets were gifts in disguise?

- What if we harvest the greatest blessings by overcoming our challenges and growing through adversity?

- What if arguing with our circumstances closes the door to learning?

- What if life is not about getting what we want, but, instead, is designed to challenge us to step into who we really are?

- What if life is not thwarting us but serving us?

- What if life is our greatest teacher, calling forward from within our next best self?

Here is a tip that has helped me so much. Something that changed everything for me as far as facing adversity. Helping me turn problems into blessings, win in my life and help my clients win in their lives. Here it is:

- There is no such thing as a problem that has no solution, once I upshift into creativity.

- Often the process of creating solutions brings blessings greater than I knew to ask for.

When I look at my life, I see this is true. Often the biggest challenges have brought the greatest blessings. Problem > Possibility > Project > Results far greater than anything that would have occurred if I hadn't met that so-called problem. I am much more than I was due to meeting life's challenges and overcoming adversity. I bet you are too.

NOW A STORY

I was in session with a client who was in a fuddle. She was married to a man she loved. They had two children they both adored, a home they had worked together to make beautiful. The problem as she saw it was, well, he wasn't financially ambitious. He made a good enough living, but for what she wanted it wasn't enough.

She had just started a program that was going to launch her into a new career. She was kinda sorta excited about it as it was going to take her to a good place. She was also resentful. She didn't want to be training for a new vocation.

My client goes on to tell me how she had dreamed of being with a man who generated enough income so she could be a stay-at-home mom. For years she had lived in unhappiness as she was currently working various part-time jobs to generate money so she could have more of what she wanted for herself and her family. This unhappiness leaked out into the mood of the family. She and her husband were perpetually in disagreement over this or that. She knew she was picking fights with him as a way to retaliate for her disappointment. She blamed him for taking away her dream of staying home with their children.

Suddenly she stopped talking. Her eyes lit up. She looked at me and said, "Oh my, I would be so bored! Instead, the financial situation is pushing me out the door to do what I love to do."

Her circumstances served in waking her up to more than her teenage fantasy of what grown-up happiness would be. I encouraged her to see her husband through new eyes. Thank-you-eyes. Thank you for being exactly as you are. Because you are as you are, I am growing into the me I want to be, even if I didn't realize how much I wanted to be that.

Shedding the old skin of the romantic fantasy of a stay-at-home mom, this woman joyously stepped forward into, for her, something even greater than that.

ই ৫ ৶ ৶ ৲ ৫

RX: Do This — Stop the Argument

- Take a moment to turn your attention inward. Let yourself come across an upset. Another way to say it is where are you not at peace. As you are still breathing there is big probability that there is some part of you upset about something. Whenever we are not in peace, we are in argument.

- Pay attention to thinking that relates to the disturbance. What is the argument? Pay attention to *should/should-not* thinking. What should be that isn't, or vise-versa?

- Allow yourself to wonder how the circumstances might be serving you in some way. How might they be asking you to shed the skin of what is familiar and expand into something more? (The guidance you are looking for may come to you at another time. Perhaps when you are washing the dishes, in a nighttime dream, or in the middle of speaking to someone. Just give the question time to simmer and see what bubbles to the surface.)

- Could you let go of expectations and discover what is *here and now?*

- Would you be willing to step into gratitude for not getting what you want?

- Might you wonder how not getting what you want might be giving you something better?

26. Love is Learning and Learning is Loving

The beautiful thing about learning is that
no one can take it away from you.

B.B. King

☙❧

Since we weren't born knowing everything about ourselves and about life, it makes sense that much of life is about learning. Which means making mistakes. Not many folks enjoy making mistakes, unless, of course, they have fallen in love with the process of learning.

Learning includes blundering and going off course. It's part of the process. We learn from making our missteps. No learning ever occurs without error. Yet many of us argue with this reality by demanding that we live without mistakes!

We could calm down about our imperfections. I, myself, have had to, and still on occasion, quell the tendency to try to be perfect in an imperfect world. But only because I don't want to live in Crazy Brain.

That means calming down in the midst of the disturbance of having veered off course. I had to learn there is no such thing as perfect; that I could grow into excellence, but perfection is a myth. One that tortures. The Perfectionist Monster can be quite cruel.

I finally realized that off course is part of the process of my learning, growth and evolution. The goal is to put in a correction as soon as possible. Once I embraced this truth, I began to calm down with the process of living on planet Earth.

One day I heard that an airplane is off course roughly 95% of the time. The sophisticated mechanisms in the cockpit keep putting in corrections, navigating the plane to its intended destination. I realized my opportunity was to develop internal mechanisms helping me to pay attention to when I was off course, so I could put in a correction as soon as possible.

This is called practice. Observing when I've engaged in an error of approach, drifted off course, failed to pay attention in some way. Putting in a correction, getting back on the path of my evolution, my choices, my intentions. Practice includes mistakes. There is no such thing as excellence without practice, error, engagement, participation.

Doing so made my focus more powerful. Instead of investing in a perfection that didn't exist, I chose, and still do, to invest in taking responsibility for my choices, paying attention to the outcome, learning from what I created, and making new choices. It's called creativity. It's called participation. It's called showing up for life.

It is also called Loving. Because judging mistakes is unkind and discouraging, it blocks learning. It is not an environment that fosters openness, curiosity and wonder.

Imagine holding your arms wide open while someone is throwing things at you. Not your natural response. Instead, you would most likely recoil in order to protect yourself from the onslaught.

Studies have shown that talking kindly to plants helps them grow and thrive. Same for all living things. That means it is true for you.

Life is messy. It doesn't have to be nasty. Nasty is when we judge ourselves for our blunders.

Judging is optional. Learning is optional. Which one are you going to choose?

ৠ ৶ ৶ ৶ ৠ ৶

RX: Do This — Love Yourself While Learning

- Be kind to you. Learn to celebrate your mistakes as evidence that you are participating in your life.

- Appreciate yourself for your willingness to take the risks that are putting you in position to make mistakes.

- When something doesn't turn out the way you intended, see if you can uncover a correction to use for next time, one that would improve the result.

- Yay you!

TIME TO PAUSE

Turn your attention within.

Notice your breathing.

Observe what is present.

Take a conscious breath into your belly.

Exhale and continue.

27. White Dot Wars

World peace must develop from inner peace.
Peace is not just the absence of violence but the
manifestation of human compassion.

The Dalai Lama

ॐ

What if someone is upset with you? You inadvertently banged into a White Dot waiting to happen and now they are blaming you for their disturbance! What's a person to do? Another chance to Calm Down and Lift Up into the awareness that their distress is not about you.

Imagine you are pollen in the air. You're just neutrally floating around, doing what pollen does. Yet your presence may start someone sneezing due to an allergic reaction.

The pollen is the perturbing finger for that person. They are set up to sneeze. Yet there are other folks who love the fragrance of you. There are others who don't even know you are there.

It's not personal when someone's upset with you. This is important for us to understand because we often imagine it's our fault. It very well may be the way they are interpreting the situation, the meaning they are assigning, is what is disturbing them.

We don't react to people, situations, or circumstances, rather we react to the meaning we are projecting onto a neutral occurrence. It is just pollen floating in the air. It's not the pollen's fault people sneeze.

NOW A STORY

I was working on a project with a man, who I will call Pete. Pete's private office was in a large room. My guess is the room was about 20'x24'. His desk was at the far end of the room. The entryway had no door. When I needed something, I would walk into the room and over to his desk. For some reason I could not grasp at the time, Pete would get upset.

As time went on and this continued to occur, I shared with him my observation that he seemed to be upset when I came into his office. Pete agreed with me that he was upset. In a tone of voice, full of irritation, he accused me of being rude and insensitive by barging into his office.

It seems I was the perturbing finger to Pete's White Dot. By the time I arrived at his desk, his upset White Dot was in full bloom and he was sneezing everywhere.

At the time, I took his disturbance personally, particularly the part where I was called rude and insensitive. I felt unjustly accused. I became defensive. Now *my* White Dot was fully engaged. You can imagine how the rest of the conversation went. It wasn't pretty.

White Dot War is no fun.

As I don't enjoy upset, and prefer peace, I was determined to Calm Down so I could Lift Up and see what was going on between us from a higher perspective. I hung out in wonder, curious as to what was happening, as I was not enjoying our interaction at all. I was tired of my White Dot getting perturbed by his accusing me for his upset.

One day I had an insight. I remembered reading a book on personal space during my undergrad schooling. Personal space is the variable and subjective distance at which one person feels comfortable interacting with another. I recalled being fascinated that people perceived the space around them differently.

The realization was that Pete and I had a different sense of personal space. Pete was born and raised in Oklahoma in a small town of 7,000 residents. The 2010 Census reported that the entire state of Oklahoma had a population of less than 4 million people with a population density of about 55 inhabitants per square mile.

I, on the other hand, was born in New York City and raised 20 miles outside of Manhattan. NYC has a population of approximately 8.5 million. That is just the City. The 2010 Census reported that the New York metropolitan area, the most populous in the United States, had a population of over 22 million. The population density was 1,865 per square mile, much higher in the City itself.

Can you guess why I am telling you this?

New Yorkers, as you may have heard, have no problem being close to each other. Visitors sometimes call New Yorkers rude and pushy. The reality is there is not much room to stand, no less spread out. In Oklahoma there is more space. Someone walking right up to you would be considered—well—rude.

My ah-ha!: Pete interpreted my behavior as impolite due to the difference in how we interpret personal space.

Was I bad-mannered?

Not if you are from New York.

This story isn't about Pete. It is about what happens when we are attached to our thinking that we are right, and the other person is wrong. We all have our Inner-Pete, the one waiting to pounce the moment the White Dot gets banged into. There is no peace, no collaboration, cooperation or fun in a relationship that is engaged in *right-wrong/good-bad* thinking. White Dot wars, running around the Hamster Wheel of Hades going nowhere.

In truth, all Pete had to do was calm down and realize there was something he wanted from me. If he was calm, he might have recognized I didn't understand that he wanted me to knock at the door (invisible as it was) and wait to be invited into his personal space. A space which extended from his desk to the opening to the room. He then could have made a request. "Moving forward I would appreciate it if you would knock at the door and wait to be invited in. Is that something you could agree to?"

The same would be true if you and I were dance partners for the first time. It is not *your* fault if you step on *my* toes not realizing I wear a size 12 shoe and I didn't tell you. (I don't. It's just a visual.) If you step on me and I call you names, well, whose job is it to take care of my big feet? It's my White Dot. It's my job to take care of me by letting you know how to dance with me so we both can enjoy the experience.

I can more easily hear your preference, or you will hear mine, if we speak from calm caring for ourselves and our relationship. One more perk of learning to lift into calm.

28. You Won't Remember This Later

I thought it was going to be a lot worse than this.

Paula Poundstone

☙❧

I remember the first time someone said to me, when I was in the midst of upset, "This too shall pass." Instead of being comforted I found myself outraged. "How dare they? Don't they know how horrible my life is right now?" Yet, whatever it was, it did pass. I don't even remember what I let disturb me to such a degree of indignation.

I've lived long enough to realize that whatever it is does pass. The positive, the negative, the everything in between comes and goes. Life is always changing, like the weather. It serves me not, nor anyone else, to be upset with the rain, snow, wind. It is equally as useless to attempt to hold onto the sunshine.

I continue to learn to let life be as it is. Giving up trying to change the direction it is going. Releasing opinions about what should or should not happen; what is right or wrong, good or bad. The Should Monster arguing with reality, yet again.

Life can be challenging, even difficult at times, but it doesn't have to be a hardship. We make it hard when we argue with our situation, when we doubt that we have the resources necessary to deal with the hand we have been dealt. We do. We have the ability to meet our circumstances and win. Look at your life. You have evidence.

NOW A STORY

A friend of mine was telling me how he handles upset in his life. He told me that four years ago he had to redo some plumbing in his historic house. When he got the estimate, he had to catch his breath. He was rattled as the cost for the repairs was daunting. He was shocked at the amount and hadn't a clue as to how he would come up with the funds.

Years later he ran into someone who asked how much the job had cost since he was facing a similar problem. My friend couldn't remember. He vaguely remembered having plumbing issues. It was over and done. He had handled it. It was long forgotten.

As a result of this encounter, he created a technique that works for him. I have tried it and it is useful. Perhaps it will work for you. When he is upset, he tells himself that he won't remember this later. That's all he does. He quietly reminds himself about the plumbing and focuses his direction elsewhere. "I'm going to forget about this later, so it doesn't matter now." This quiets his frantic, fretting *worry-brain,* putting the *upsetting* situation in perspective. Reminding himself he won't remember it later allows him to deal with

148 • Leslie Sann

whatever it is as trivial, which in the big picture it really is. The Worry Monster fades into the background and The Creative Mind steps in.

Years ago, there was a book called, *Don't Sweat the Small Stuff. It's all Small Stuff.* What if the broken plumbing, the divorce, the job loss, the defiant child, is all small stuff? In the scheme of things, it's just life happening. There's no need to stress about bumps in the road; it's just part of the journey. If you need to, put your seatbelt on, but keep driving.

ANOTHER STORY

I have a close relative who is experiencing short-term memory loss. During a recent visit I experienced my own version of Groundhog Day. (Did you see that movie? It's a good one.)

If we had any friction that may have irritated my White Dot, I reminded myself she wasn't going to remember this in about 5 minutes so I may as well forget it too. This reminder helped me let go of my upset, moving me quickly into forgiving and forgetting. If she wasn't going to remember, well, I didn't have to either. The benefit was there was more space for me to wonder what I could do better next time as our relationship was in new terrain. That trip was one of the most enjoyable and relaxing visits I have ever had with her. The key — forget the upset and carry on.

Life is always on the move. You've been on the planet Earth long enough to know this is true. Everything changes here. Perhaps it is time to learn to be with what is.

ꝗ ꝓ ꝓ ꝙ ꝗ ꝓ

RX: Do This — Call Yourself Present to *Now*, to *Here*

- Breathe into your belly. Relax. Invite yourself into patience. Life will unfold as it does. It always has, it always will, whether you like it or not. Accept or argue, we are not in control.

- What you are in charge of is your relationship with the part of you that argues, that is frightened, that doubts. Embrace the disturbance. Be still. Let it be. The upset will relax and quiet. Shift your focus to look for the good. What is the opportunity here? Perhaps you are learning about patience, how strong you are, what endurance truly is.

- One step, then the next.

- Inhale. Exhale.

- That's all that is required.

- In the quiet you will find you are quite resourceful. You will figure something out. You always do.

- It is the doing that does it.

Simple, yes. Easy — well — Rome wasn't built nor did it burn in a day. It takes time to dismantle old patterns and create space for the new to arise. We don't go to the gym once and expect to go home looking like bodybuilders. We know muscles don't work that way. Brain science tells us that over time, with repetitive neurological action, you can change your brain. With practice, simple may become easy.

29. Where You Are Powerful

You have more power than you realize.

Elastigirl — Mom Incredible

ᘏᗴ

We are creators and our life is our work of art, our creation. Just like a painter who creates with a palette of color which is limited by the color spectrum of light, humans striving to create and design our own lives are also limited. Limitation doesn't mean lack. Limitation inspires creativity through focus, discernment and attention.

These 'colors' are NOT our palette, as in we canNOT control:

The past

Our feelings

Our bodies

Random thoughts

Other people's feelings

The future

Other people's choices and actions

There are only TWO colors on our palette. That may not seem like much. Yet, with these two things, we are VERY POWERFUL!

They are — (drum roll please):

Our choices

and

Our actions

TA DA!

That's it.

To me this is good news. Now we know what is a waste of our precious time, resources and energy. With this information we can shift into investing in that which will actually reap a useful reward.

Your choices and actions are

what make you powerful.

Shift your focus from dwelling in the past. Forget about other people's thinking, feeling and behavior. Don't hold onto what you are thinking and feeling. Stop doing what you don't want to do and do something else. Choose new actions that bring you joy and leave the rest alone.

We have no power or control over what people think. It is, therefore, better to invest in something we can direct. Such as being the person we choose to be and investing in making today a good day.

The Stoics believe that living well, as in having material abundance, is very different from having a good life. The attempt to possess or control that which is not on our palette will not secure inner peace. It will not protect us from loss or hardship. Many live in upset and unhappiness in a world of plenty. Our sense of well-being is what matters.

Tranquility is fostered from within. Peace is a practice. The world naturally draws us into disturbance. Life is designed to be upsetting. If you value tranquility then make peace a practice, an ongoing focus and commitment.

ꙫ ꙮ ꙭ ꙭ ꙫ ꙮ

RX: Do This — Out-There to In-Here

- We have no power over Out-There (other people, situations, circumstances). Consider this: might you be better served investing in something over which you have control? Perhaps investing in being the person you choose to be, creating a life you love and investing in making today a good day?

- You change because of how you choose to take new action.

Suggestion: Invest in what you have control over, *you*. Design a practice — *one* thing you could do consistently over the next week that will help you shift up into peace and presence. If you like the results, do it again for another week, until it becomes your new uplifting, upshifted habit.

Examples:

- Slowing down to the speed limit when driving.

- Eliminating devices at the dinner table, or elsewhere, when you are in a social situation.

- Smiling at strangers, at friends, gosh, at anyone.

- No snacking after 7:30 PM, supporting restorative sleep

- Turning the text dinger off so you are not a Pavlov's dog to the stimulus.

- Contacting someone to thank them for something they did to make your life better.

- Pausing to take five conscious breaths periodically throughout the day.

- Doing something today that will positively contribute to your future, such as investing 10% of your paycheck, walking an extra block, calling a friend you haven't connected with in some time.

Just some examples. What do you imagine could be useful to you?

30. Magoo Madness

How you relate to your life IS your life.

Ron Hulnick

ॐ

Life on planet Earth Ha-Ha. With life doing what it does and me contributing to the chaos, it's an amusing ride. Magoo Madness.

For those of you who don't know where the word Magoo comes from, Quincy Magoo (or simply Mr. Magoo) is a cartoon character created in 1949. You could google Mr. Magoo and watch a few of the cartoons. Wherever Mr. Magoo went, calamity happened. The humor was that Mr. Magoo seemed to be exempt from any distress himself.

Allow me to share a week of Magoo Madness in the life of moi.

NOW A STORY

I tossed my phone, which was in a red case, on top of the laundry basket, knowing that once I get downstairs, I would do my usual sort, thus my phone will be taken out of the clothes pile. But, for some reason that didn't happen. Magoo Madness took over. Since everything in the basket was dark, I dumped the whole thing into the washing machine. Not my usual pattern.

It wasn't until I got up the stairs back into the kitchen that I realized the phone was in the washing machine. By the time I retrieved it, water had entered the charging portal. I watched the screen turn to wavy lines. I began to shake it. Water came out of the portal. Excited that I might be able to save the phone, I shook it even harder. Alas, my reward was watching the screen go black. The phone was officially dead.

There was nothing to do to resurrect Lazarus; I mean my phone from the dead. The next day, I purchased a replacement. On my way home that night, driving in the near pitch-black darkness of a country road, a skunk appeared in my headlights. I swerved so that he could live another day. It seemed the skunk had other plans. He decided to throw himself under the wheels of my car. Leaving with a departing gift!

Skunk stink is quite a phenomenon. The reek was so bad it filled up my garage and started oozing into the house. Next day I drove through a car wash hoping to *wash that smell right out of my car and send it on its way.*

Nope. Though better, the smell lingered. A sickly-sweet smell that made me nauseous.

Hi-Ho-Hi-Ho, off to the auto detailing shop I go. They've seen this before. Half hour later I'm back in my car driving home only to realize they replaced the stink of skunk with the aroma of air freshener. It smelled worse than the skunk. At least the skunk came from nature. That pine smelling whatever was a chemical and it was driving me batty.

I called the detail shop. The woman who answered apologized for not asking beforehand if it was okay to use the air-freshener. She promised if I left all the windows open, the smell would be gone in 10 minutes.

Three days later the smell lingered.

Oh ... my new gynecologist's nurse called me the next day to talk about the results of a test in the light of my hysterectomy. Ummm, I haven't had a hysterectomy.

Magoo-Madness!

Let's just shorten that to Magoo-ness. Life on planet Earth, unfolding however it does, whether I want it to go that way or not.

My choice after this week of silliness was go to laughter instead of to upset. What a world we live in! Life going left when I thought it was going right — skunks in the road, cell phones in the washing machine, inaccurate medical records — launching me in a different direction than I had planned. *Life happens* other than planned — *now what?*

I know a woman who lost her home in a fire. A few days later I saw her beaming, a big smile on her face. Do you know what she said? "It is only stuff."

Not everything can be laughed at right away, yet our opinion about what should've been happening can be let go. Life is as it is. From our limited point of view, it may seem like madness. It's not personal. Just life, fires, skunks doing what they do.

What happens to you when the unexpected shows up? How do you react? How do you relate to the issue?

I do not have freedom to control my circumstances or how other people or skunks show up in my world. When I choose to participate in creating what I want I am authoring my life. In Middle English, *author* means "someone who invents or causes something." As author of my life, I create the story I tell. How I choose to be in relationship to people, circumstances and skunks is the experience I get to live in.

This is what Calm Down Lift Up looks like for me: Meeting life on life's terms, I navigate Magoo-ness with joy, laughter, smiles and a grateful heart.

If misadventure can become a funny story later, I may as well enjoy it while it is happening. I choose to keep rewiring my brain to lift up into joy and laughter as my response to the unexpected.

Join me?

31. Failing Forward

*'Failure' is just a label someone made up to
identify an experience of not getting what they
wanted when and where they wanted it.*

John-Roger

༄༅

Our culture has made the word *fail* a big deal. As if failing is something to be feared. This fear disappears when we see failure as not getting what we want, when we want it.

I fail, so what? I don't get what I want. It happens every day. It is the nature of life on the planet.

I'm imagining you have heard the expression, "What would you do if you could not fail?" It's a pithy encouragement to take risks. Yet, in fact, we do fail. Probably daily. We quite often don't get what we want.

How useful is it to imagine what it would be like to not fail? A more empowering focus, to me, is what is the gift of failure? How does not getting what I want serve me?

Not getting what I want, when and where I want it, has often been a gift. A gift of learning, of growth. Sometimes, it is the gift of making space so something even better than I had imagined could appear. It's all about how I relate to the moment of not getting. Seeing it as a *for me* experience assists me in engaging creatively. Creativity is how I partner with life.

Failure does happen. So what? *Now what?*

Instead of asking "what if I could not fail?" perhaps it would be useful to ask:

- What didn't work?

- Why not?

- What can I learn as a result of what occurred?

- What can I do differently next time?

- Is there a gift in not getting what I thought I wanted?

- What doors of possibility are now open to me?

- *Now what?*

How many times have you frozen out of fear of failure (or rejection) rather than take a next step? Action is what produces results. Without action there is no creation.

Mistakes are an intrinsic part of the process of learning, growth, and evolution. Mistakes are neutral. They're not a condemnation as our Crazy Brains try to make us believe. They're just information, an opportunity, if we choose to take it.

Mistakes tell us it is time to pause and reevaluate what we are doing. It seems we have strayed off course. No big deal. Time to put in a correction and get back on the path — make new choices, take new actions.

Three steps forward and two steps back is still forward progress. We *fail forward* if we keep choosing to participate, pay attention, put in corrections, and learn from experience what works and what doesn't.

We *fail forward* IF we keep going. And that's the key to life in everything we do: keep on keepin' on. Keep showing up.

Stand back up once more after you fall down. Standing up is part of learning.

How to make the journey easier? Pay attention. Notice when there's been a drift off course. Put in a correction as soon as possible. The more quickly we do so, the more easefully, gracefully and expediently we will meet our goal.

This is not about right or wrong or good or bad. Mistakes are just information. Yet for too many of us the Mind Monster that specializes in judgment and blame creeps out from under the bed and pounces, reprimanding the *mistake* or misstep. The misstep could be choosing to marry someone, going for a job, moving to a new location, investing in a company, and finding the situation going other than planned. Failure? Not the way I look at life. Classroom? Yes. But only if you pay attention to the teacher.

Judging is not useful. The Judging Monster is yet another way we suffer our minds. It diminishes rather than increases our ability to observe and see where we can make useful corrections. It takes us down versus lifting us up so we can see further from a higher perspective, a greater altitude, enabling us to see where we may have gone off course. What can be done differently now?

We can choose to lift up by:

- taking a few breaths

- calming the chattering brain

- expanding into quiet

- observing the situation as if watching the actions unfold on a screen

- neutrally witnessing with curiosity and wonder

- noticing what didn't work, why, and what is now possible

When we pause, quiet and lift so we can see what isn't working — without judgment — we are available to creative alternatives. The sooner we observe and make a correction, the sooner we get back on the path to where we want to go, including moving to a place of peace within.

Observe and correct. Off course. On course. Just like a plane putting in corrections throughout the journey so it arrives at the intended destination.

Life doesn't unfold in a straight line either. Learn to utilize your own navigational tools, as in learning from *mistakes,* so you get to where you want to go, at peace throughout the journey, participating one step at a time.

ॠ ℘ ℘ ॡ ॠ ℘

RX: Do This — Fun with the Letters F A I L

- **F**irst **A**ttempt **I**n **L**earning. Mistakes or missteps are part of the process of growth. There really is no failure other than the choice to stop participating. Don't give up. Keep going.

- **F**un **A**lways **I**n **L**aughter. We can always teehee ourselves through anything. Laughter upshifts us into the creative brain. Studies show you cannot think and laugh at the same time. Therefore, according to moi, laughter is the antidote to misery. Even if we are faking it, the brain can't tell the difference and will flood the system with endorphins and dopamine. That kind of cocktail brings an ease to life that is delicious and useful. From ease we open yet again to our creative, resourceful brain.

- **Finding An Important Lesson.** Mistakes are an indication there is an opportunity for learning. A sign we are off course. There is an error in approach, and it might be wise to experiment with something new.

There is no such thing as failure.

We fail in the direction we are going.

Get up and keep going.

Just the next step.

And then the one after that.

32. Ingenious Magoo

Creativity is inventing, experimenting, growing, taking risks, breaking rules, making mistakes, and having fun.

Mary Lou Cook

ॐ

The fun of Mr. Magoo is that he is always running into things because he is extremely nearsighted and he refuses to get glasses. As a result, things happen that could have been avoided IF he had been paying attention.

A Magoo Moment is the result of having pulled a Magoo. Meaning you weren't present or paying attention, and something happened.

For example, the first time you ran out of gas because you weren't attending to the gas gauge and — oops — to the side of the road you go. Or that time the bathtub overflowed, or you forgot where you put your keys, or sent an email with personal information to the wrong person.

Or for me, it was leaving my wallet at home only to realize it when I was 54 miles away from the wallet with no chance to retrieve it for hours and hours.

Oh Drat! (or something like that). I had no money.

All of a sudden, I amusingly became very hungry as I realized I was facing 8+ hours of no food.

I took a breath or two (or more) and calmed down. I let myself go empty as I opened in wonder. *What am I going to do about this?* I let the brain do its thing and, like the good search engine it is, it began to offer me solutions to my problem.

What about Apple Pay?

No go. I have not as yet used it and the credit card I had entered was expired.

Hmmm, call the credit card company and ask for help.

No go again. With all the security measures that didn't go well.

I could also fast. That is actually a healthy choice.

Naw ... I'm working with clients all day and I want my blood sugar to be stable.

Hmmm, how can I create some money?

Search-Search-Search goes the brain.

Search Engine Win: TA DA! I realize that there is a stash of quarters in my car for meters and toll booths (from when the meters and the toll booths were only taking coins). I added them up and had enough to get something to eat. While I wasn't going to be dining on steak, my blood sugar would be okay.

By the time I got to my Chicago office, I had created even more cash. Way more than was needed. (That was fun.)

While searching my internal computer for a solution to the problem, I was designing new systems for the future to catch me if this ever happened again. As of this writing, not only is my credit card in my Apple Pay useful, I actually know how to use it. I also have money in my car for unexpected needs. And, I put other safety measures in place, including *finishing* what

I start. The wallet was at home because I stopped paying attention and failed to put it in my purse. I pulled a Magoo.

Life happens. Sometimes we instigate our own troubles. We have our Magoo moments. I generally will innovate out of Magoo-isms. I teach myself to pay more attention and I design a new system that will serve me going forward.

I bet you do that too.

We are human becomings, learning and growing as we evolve into *next*. If you pay attention to where plans go astray, you can design actions and implement new behavior to serve you.

Humans love to create solutions. It is part of the human design. The human brain is hardwired to solve problems. Thus, we see obstacles everywhere. Bummer is we pay more attention to the fact that we have difficulties rather than focusing on the fun of working things out.

By the way, have you seen my blue scarf? It seems to have gone missing. Methinks Mrs. Magoo hid it from me.

P.S. Magoo Madness is part of life on planet Earth. Have you ever had a Magoo moment? Wanna tell me about it? Write to me, I love hearing about our shared humanity, the challenges, the wins and the sillies. Send your stories to: leslie@living-bydesign.com. I promise not to tell.

33. WOW Brain

Turn agitation to curiosity to wonder.

༄

Living in Wide Open Wonder (W O W) is the antidote to Crazy Brain. Wonder opens us to creativity.

I wonder ... hmmm?

Through reflection and wonder we grow in wisdom, harvesting what has gone before, especially when we ask the questions, *How has this served me? What can I learn from this? If I want to do better, what can I do?*

Wisdom is using those things that work for us as long as they work for us, while letting go of what is no longer working. Wonder opens us to perceiving our reality in new ways. It assists us in accessing our ability to invent, innovate and create.

When we find ourselves in Crazy Brain, running around the Hamster Wheel of Hades going nowhere, we have a choice. We can choose to be responsible. Responsibility is the Doorway to Heaven. It is the portal into Wonder Brain.

I love playing with words. The word *responsibility* is the ability to respond. If we have the ability to respond, we have the power to make a choice. This is where true freedom is. This is the Doorway to Heaven.

When we are in Crazy Brain we are in reactivity. Reactivity is fine. Life happens and we react. No big deal.

Scramble the letters in *reactivity* and create the word *creativity*. Do you see it? Better yet, do it. Doing it requires a wonder question. The question to ask is, *Now what?*

Now what shifts our focus from problem to possibility. Something happening is an opportunity to be creative. Designing something new out of what has occurred. *Now what* opens the mind to inspiration.

Now what? What am I going to do about it?

Crazy Brain is hell, the Hamster Wheel of Hades kind of hell. We just keep running around, running around, triggering ourselves into more upset, going nowhere. Until we decide to do something about it. That moment of decision is when we take responsibility. We choose to respond.

We decide to upshift by accessing our freedom of choice.

This is the power we have as human beings. We have the ability to choose.

There are some things we cannot control. Gravity for example. Yet we can choose to be creative in the face of how life is designed. Think of sports. Playing with gravity. Ball goes up, ball comes down. Sports are an example of being creative with what is.

We have power with our choices and actions. That is freedom. Once we step through the Doorway to Heaven, we ask a wonder question, "Hmmm ... *now what?"* — and the creative brain opens up. We don't even have to know what to do. Just open and allow the creativity to begin to percolate.

We begin to upshift when we open the WOW brain (Wide Open Wonder.) All of a sudden, we get an idea. We are inspired. Where did that inspiration come from? Spirit. We become receptive to Divine Intelligence, the Magnificent Mystery. We bring that information through our human creativity and design new ways of being. A gift of our humanity.

There's nothing else on the planet that does this: imagines a future, references the past, and takes action to create something new. From those actions humans create a future that wasn't there before. In the beginning there were no such things as cooked food, houses, or iPhones. We created all that.

Amazing us.

What if the world is *designed* to be upsetting? What if, rather than giving us what we want, life is challenging us to *lift* into who we are?

I have asked participants in my workshops, clients, friends, neighbors, if their lives turned out the way they had imagined. I haven't found a person yet who has said, "Yes." Most have said their life has turned out even better. Not what was imagined, *even better.* Better because they discovered they were *more* than they had imagined. And so are you.

Like in Chapter 6, dancing with the elephant is the way to go. Engaging from wonder takes us to *even better.* Discovering that we will endure until the end, that we can handle what life gives us, shows us what we are really made of. This is the source of joy.

Imagine life getting even better.

W O W.

34. Breathe into Peace

*I keep trying to catch up with my breath while my
breath patiently waits for me to slow down.*

Martha Ringer

ᘒᗷ

Life does happen and often it is upsetting or disturbing to
our status quo. The first thing our body does is to get upset or
disturbed. Of course, it does. The body wants to live another
day, so it goes into fight-or-flight!

Yet, you can change the way you react to stress. Research
has discovered that it isn't the stressor itself, but rather our
response to that stress that creates disturbance.

We cannot do much, if anything, about outer circum-
stances, situations or people. But we can do something about
how we respond to the experience we are having. That's good
news.

One of the ways we can take care of ourselves in the face
of stress is to learn how to breathe properly. As babies we in-
stinctively know how to do this. Babies breathe with their
whole bodies, their stomachs puffing out every time they
breathe in and collapsing when they breathe out.

Check your own breathing. Place one hand on your chest
and the other on your stomach, then take a normal breath.

What happened to your hands? Did they even move? Which moved more?

If you're like most people, neither moved much. For many, the chest moves more. That's the habit of shallow breathing.

You can use deep breathing to counter the fight-or-flight reaction any time you feel stressed. Practice noticing your breath and when you catch yourself shallow breathing, take time to take your breath into your belly and breathe deeply.

Shifting your breathing is a powerful antidote to the knee-jerk response many of us have to the ongoing bombardment of things to do and places to be.

It's easier to learn to breathe deeply when you are in a calm situation. I suggest a daily 10-minute breathing practice will exercise the diaphragm and support the body in its ability to breathe deeply under stress.

Next time you find yourself irate because of an unexpected traffic jam, or are rushing to meet a deadline, or are rehearsing your request for a raise, practice deep breathing and calm yourself down.

Conscious breathing is a powerful, soothing influence. We use the breath to call ourselves present into peace. Calming down is one of the most, if not *the* most, important skills we can learn. This is the reason I wrote this book. This is also why I have created the companion *Calm Down Lift Up* online learning program.

One reason I love BreathWork is because it is an expedient path to calming down. From *calm* we have access to the well of our being, filled with tools and resources. We don't have to figure anything out before we get to the moment. We can trust, in each moment, that everything we need is available.

Using breath to calm is a graceful and easy process of getting out of our heads and into our lives. From this place you have access to creative resources beyond your mind's ability to imagine: inspiration reveals itself; innovation and invention are birthed; problems are seen as possibilities and actions are designed to bring those possibilities into reality.

You can breathe yourself into peace.

You can do it right now.

How?

Inhale — now exhale — on purpose.

Observe the breath.

Listen to the sound as the air moves in and out.

Let the sound be a calming influence.

Inhale into your belly.

Let the breath expand up into your upper chest.

Release the breath — and then inhale.

That's it.

Feel the pleasure of your lungs expanding and contracting.

Let the pleasure and the sound relax you even more.

You got it.

Notice the quiet in between the sounds — let the quiet expand.

Ahh ...

Better, yes?

Calming down, coming present into *now*.

Life happens.

Now what?

Breathe.

We are more creative when we are calmly focused on what is possible. We are always in the middle of life happening. It serves us to calm down so we can meet *what is* with our creative power.

NOW A STORY

Sitting in the profound quiet that occurs after a BreathWork session, I wait in the stillness for my client to speak what is present. She tells me she feels enormous. "I am huge. You are part of this with me."

I wait.

I want her to have the space for her experience to deepen.

It is true. We are enormous. There really is no end to the essence of who we are. And we are the same.

The breath that breathes me, breathes you. We are being breathed together.

I suggest she imagine an ocean. At the surface of the ocean are waves. Now imagine identifying as a wave. The sense of *individual* happens based on where we are looking. We look out over the sea at other waves and conclude they are separate.

Not true.

All waves are of one ocean.

We are of one breath.

There is no true separation, only what the mind imagines.

Waves come and go, and the ocean remains. Waves arise out of the ocean and return again. Life moving, flowing, changing shape, yet at essence the same.

When we turn our attention from Out-There looking at other waves, and shift our awareness to the breath, to That Which Breathes Us, it becomes clear we are connected and the same.

My client loved that image and allowed it to seep into her bones.

Coming out of the BreathWork session restored and renewed was like flowing back into the Ocean of Oneness. At the depth of the quiet within, a next action for her life was revealed. Now back at the surface she will ride the inspiration received to the shore through action.

> In/Out
>
> Receive/Express
>
> In/Out
>
> Gather/Give
>
> In/Out

We are being breathed.

Peace is a practice. The world naturally draws us into disturbance. The world itself is disturbing. If you value tranquility, make it a practice, an ongoing focus and commitment to practice peace.

You can access peace through the breath.

Take time each day and tune yourself in to the peace of your presence inside of you. Then bring that peace out into your life. Don't look for a result or a reward. Just do the best you can to be a peaceful presence throughout your day, throughout your life.

The peace that you are, the peace that you live, the peace that you give, is your reward. Peace is who you truly are. Allow it to flow through you. Recognize it as a gift you give, first to yourself, then to others and into our world.

This world could use a giant dose of peace.

ॺ ๕ ๒ ๒ ๖ ๕

RX: Do This — Breathe Yourself Calm

- Start each day — before you even put your feet on the floor — by taking one minute to sit up and take a minimum of five easy, relaxed breaths.

- Note how you begin to feel. This initial feeling sets the tone for the day.

- Settle into the breathing until you are in a place where you want to start your day. You are be-ginning your day with intention and breath.

- As you move throughout the day, when you begin to feel pressed, over-scheduled, or out of the moment, relax again into your breathing.

- Do this as often as you need during the day.

- At the end of the day, reflect on whether this made a difference for you.

- If not, don't be discouraged, continue with the experiment tomorrow. Stay committed to the practice of calming down.

- Breathe yourself calm.

- Be peace.

I welcome you to consider the experience of Breath-Work as a next step. Private BreathWork sessions with me can be facilitated in person, via videoconference or by phone. The details can be found here: www.breathworkwithleslie.com

35. Is There a Message in Disturbance?

Life goes by fast. Enjoy it. Calm down.
It's all funny. Next.

Joan Rivers

༄༅

One of the ways we grow ourselves is by loving ourselves. Learning to love this unique configuration of human life. This particular human design called you.

When we are upset, we can choose self-love. We calm the upset, as if it were a crying baby, by paying attention to it. We bring our attention to that which is upset. Curious. Open. In wonder. What's going on? What is this upset about?

Sometimes it is just the Mind Monsters growling for some food. Ignoring the hungry Monsters may not work. They could just get louder and more demonstrative. They could call in re-inforcements.

What if, like a child on the ground in a full-blown tantrum, they are calling out for attention? Perhaps the upset is bringing us a message.

I remember a time I woke up in the night, anxious. Startled and now fully awake I tracked the feeling to the thinking. I became aware I was fretting because of not paying my phone bill. (That was back in the day when you had to remember to pay your bills.) In that instance, my upset was a messenger.

The anxiety was tapping me on the shoulder attempting to get my attention. I thanked the messenger, got out of bed, found my checkbook. I wrote out the check and put it in a stamped envelope to post the next day. With a now quiet mind, I tucked in and fell quickly back to sleep.

Ignoring this anxiety would not have served me. Sometimes our feelings and thoughts can be used as guiding mechanisms to keep us on track. Listening to the anxiety brought important information to my awareness. I had failed to pay my phone bill. Message received. Phone bill paid. Connection to the world stays uninterrupted. Credit remains good.

Other times anxious feelings have to do with future thinking such as worrying. Worrying is another version of fear. Fretting about something that has not yet occurred. Thinking about thinking about thinking. Pretending all that thinking is somehow useful to avoid an imagined dreaded future.

I could be anxious about my mom living by herself at this point in her life, worrying she might fall. Alone, what might happen to her? Now the disturbing feelings have my attention. What am I going to DO about it? Doing matters. Paying my phone bill mattered.

In this instance, I can turn worry into useful action. My mother now wears a Life Alert. She has also created a ritual where when she comes home, she hangs up her keys on a hook and puts the monitor around her neck. This is a comfort to her, to my sister, and to me.

Earlier I wrote about driving an hour and a half in a snowstorm. The anxiety and fretting moved me out the door sooner than I had scheduled. The result was I arrived at the venue in front of the storm.

Learning to Calm Down and Lift Up is not a spiritual by-pass. It is not about ignoring stressful thoughts, pretending nothing is going on when something is actually going on. If I am driving and the gas light appears, I don't worry I'm going to run out of gas without doing anything to avert that outcome. At the same time, I don't calm down by chanting affirmations about miraculously arriving at my destination on an empty tank. Either choice would be silly. Instead, I design a solution to my problem. I look for a gas station. I fill up my tank.

The disturbing emotion can be seen as the warning light indicating the gas is low. It is an alert attempting to get our attention, letting us know something is amiss.

I have a client who is dealing with a difficult boss. The situation seems to be somewhat of an inquisition. The boss's behavior is accusatory and threatening with no substantiating evidence. My client's upset about the situation is calling her into action. In this situation, action looks like consulting a lawyer.

Another client is working in collaboration with someone who becomes controlling when she gets anxious. This controlling behavior on the part of her partner is becoming irritating to my client. My client realizes the irritation is a message that she needs to do something. She is learning to make requests, thus leading the relationship into a better direction for them both.

Upset is not bad. Disturbance opens the door to opportunities for learning and growth. We calm down to lift into the part of us that knows how to design creative action. That is hardly spiritual bypass.

I'm not telling you to breathe yourself into peace and then go out into the world chanting Hare Krishna. Instead, I'm inviting you to realize that upset happens and what you can do about it is to make good use of it. Engage with it as it is: a doorway to your next best. Part of the process of your personal evolution.

NOW A STORY

This is a story about a trip to Italy. I went with my mother and my sister to visit the Chianti countryside and Florence for a little over one week. We had lots of laughs and an overall good time.

A month before we were to leave, Alitalia canceled the Milan to Florence leg of our trip. Too bad on us. No alternatives offered. That left us in Milan when we wanted to be south of Florence. We decided we'd take the train to Florence, pick up our car rental and handle the unexpected.

Life is what happens when you are making other plans.

One week out from our trip I began to feel anxious about this part of our journey. For some reason finding the bus that took us to downtown Milan, so we could find the train station, buy tickets, get to the track, travel to Florence, walk to the car rental place, and then drive to the farmhouse we rented, put me on edge. It seemed like too much to do after a long overseas trip. Plus, none of us speak Italian.

I suggested we drive. Let's just pick up our car rental in Milan and drive to our destination. It'll get us there at least two hours earlier than if we took the plane, bus, train, and then car. It was a go. We decided to drive the 3 hours and 48 minutes I was told the trip would take.

We found each other with little incident — they were traveling from New York and I from Chicago — and picked up our car rental. A stick shift of course. We were in Italy. Once we figured out that the light on the dashboard meant the parking brake was engaged, we were off.

TEN hours later we arrived at our destination. We had been in bumper to bumper traffic for most of the trip. Bumper to bumper driving a stick shift after an overseas flight. How fun is that?!

You might imagine that someplace down the road one of us said something like, *We could have taken the train.*

When we arrived, the owners of our accommodations acknowledged, "Yes, today is not a good day to drive." It turned out that the upcoming Tuesday was a national holiday, and *everyone* was taking a four-day vacation and going somewhere!

She informed us there was no room on the trains which were booked to capacity. Everyone who wasn't driving somewhere that day was *taking the train!* Had we chosen the train, we would have been in the station for the rest of the day, until the next morning, or longer. Even though the trip seemed like a nightmare, the original plan would have been much worse.

I have learned to love my feelings. My anxiety was a message telling me something was off course. Once we agreed to drive, my agitation calmed.

Our feelings are often messengers if we listen. They can be guides to taking action. Pay the phone bill, call your friend, go for a walk, choose another route for your travel. And most importantly, love your feelings, and love yourself.

TIME TO PAUSE

Stretch your arms above your head.

Take a gentle inhale.

On the exhale bring your arms down

while releasing any disturbance

that may be present.

Turn your attention within.

Notice your breathing.

Observe what is present.

Exhale and continue.

36. It Doesn't Matter

*Between stimulus and response there is a space. In
that space is our power to choose our response.
In our response lies our growth and our freedom.*

Viktor Frankl

❧

Oh fun, oral surgery, ow. I had a tooth that, according to the surgeon, had been traumatized at some point in my life. It was doing this odd thing called reabsorption. It was eating itself from the inside out. Dentists don't know why this happens and don't know how to arrest the process. The only option is to take the tooth out and replace it with an implant. Not a fun idea. Yet, having my tooth break while enjoying a meal was less inviting. So out the tooth went.

It turns out I wasn't the only one having oral surgery. In the next several weeks I ran into three other people in the middle of oral surgery. One of whom was also dealing with a reabsorption issue. Funny how that happens. Buy a new car and suddenly the same model car shows up all over the place.

Oh, that's a whole other topic. This is about *something happening* during the surgery. It was less than optimal and rather horrifying to me. The surgeon was putting in the implant support and — uh — the screw went through my jaw. Eek!

I was to wait three weeks until my mouth healed. At that time, the surgeon could discern the true consequence of the oops.

Until that appointment, I had to pay attention to where I was paying my attention. If I drifted into thinking about what the doctor could have/should have done instead of what he did do, I could make myself miserable. I could start fantasizing worst case scenarios. Screw through my jaw. My mind could go off into terrible outcomes. I know. I've done it. I've made myself miserable by fretting. More than once. More than twice ...

This was a ripe situation for a Crazy Brain take-over. It would have been easy to scare myself, anger myself, and make myself crazed on the way to the next dental appointment.

I do not know the *why* of this event. I have learned over the years that searching for a *why* is a way I distract myself. It buffers the experience of uncertainty and the awareness that I am not in control. It is an attempt to control what I cannot control.

Even if I figured out the *reason,* how would that serve me? I am still facing *what is.* Whatever the reason for the experience we are having — well — *it doesn't matter.*

And that is what I told myself, "It doesn't matter."

And it didn't.

There was nothing I could do to change my current situation. Could have, should have, ought-tos were worthless to me. *It doesn't matter* turned out to be an effective way to come back into this moment. *Here and now.* Now is all I could participate in. The future didn't exist, nor did the past. Future or past didn't matter. Right now is all that mattered.

It doesn't matter works great for me. When I catch my mind blah-blah-blahing about nothing, or fretting about the future when I can't take action, just yet — I sweetly tell myself it doesn't matter. Calling myself present. Calming me down.

This is a powerful tool for me. I stop thinking and shift up to witnessing the nonsense mental chatter that can be incessant. Something that gets *me* to stop thinking is, well, quite miraculous. Especially when life is doing other than I planned and my mind is trying to control reality by thinking.

Bottom line, it really doesn't matter. What my mind thinks about what is, is irrelevant. What is, is. Thus, a gentle reminder that *it doesn't matter,* quiets the mind and lifts me up. I come present and move to *next.* Lovely.

Fast forward. I'm fine. I was always fine. There was nothing to worry about at all.

I encourage you to play with this. What about you? What kind of propaganda is your mind promoting that in truth doesn't matter?

37. Rising Above It

When you change your attitude, you change your experience. When you raise your altitude on any given situation you see it with a new attitude.

Bertrand Babinet

ॐ

I recently was talking to my wise friend and health advisor. We were exploring neck discomfort I sometimes experience. He was testing to discover what, if any, remedy was available to alleviate the complaint.

I heard myself tell him that it doesn't really bother me that much because I am able to rise above it. It wasn't until later that I realized that is what I do. I lift up to a higher, more observing consciousness and witness that there is a disturbance in my body.

This is called getting altitude. Changing my point of view. Lifting to see through new eyes. From a higher place we can assess a broader scope of the problem. I am no longer in the problem but observing the problem.

From a higher perspective I might even discover it's not a problem at all. I could realize it's actually an opportunity to take care of myself in new and more rewarding ways. Which is what I am doing. I'm now on a homeopathic protocol that will help me resolve the neck discomfort.

A complaint is a signal we send ourselves in order to get our attention. Something is off course and we need to take remedial action.

If I wasn't the person who tends to rise above things (I don't always do that right away — being human and all), I could get stuck in the discomfort of my neck and begin to fret about a future in a neck brace, or some worry-brain outcome of doom and gloom. Instead, I had the wisdom to use the discomfort as motivation to take action.

Rising above it can be used when we are having conflict with another person, or are stuck in traffic, or anything that's upsetting. Practice lifting up into the place called the Witness or the Observer. Take a breath, invite yourself to relax, and from the quiet within, notice what's occurring.

Conscious Awareness Lifting Me up.

This isn't a spiritual bypass. We're not pretending that there is nothing happening. We're shifting our viewing point so we have space to assess how to intervene.

When we Calm Down and Lift Up, we have greater access to our wisdom and creative resources. It becomes clearer to us if there is an action to take, such as calling our favorite health practitioner, singing a song or taking a nap.

38. Monster to Ally

*Do I not destroy my enemies when
I make them my friends?*

Abraham Lincoln

ༀ

The truth about the Monsters is that they are doing their best to serve you. If they knew better, they would do better. Just like the Wizard, it wasn't until he was forced to give up the gig and come out from behind the curtain that he realized his methods weren't serving anyone, including himself.

Consider the Monsters well-meaning but ignorant. They are doing their best to protect and guide you safely through life. Sometimes ignoring them works. They go away. And if their voices are insistent, you have another choice. You can turn and welcome the noise.

You cannot transform what you do not embrace. With loving acceptance, turn and meet what is. Make space for the feelings that are aroused. Listen to what all the fuss is about.

Sometimes I listen to the inner mind-chatter and realize I'm whining. I say out loud, *Whiney, whiney victim, victim,* with affection. Then I listen more deeply to what that part of me really wants. It usually wants me to advocate for something. I receive the message and decide if that action serves my concerns. If so, I move into action.

Once I hear the whiney part, it calms down. I have received the message and am handling the problem.

The Inner Critic wants to keep me safe. The Should Monster does too. The key is not to make the Monster wrong. The goal is to teach it a better way of doing things. I've taught the Should Monster to be gentler by changing *should* to *could.* When I hear *should,* I remind myself the word is *could* and then I lift into choices and possibility.

What if you begin to see the Monsters not as bullies but as friends who could use some relationship skills? If you slowed down to listen more closely to their messages, you might find they are not Monsters, but rather allies. Mahatma Gandhi suggested, "Whenever you are confronted with an opponent, conquer him with love." Hmmm, what might that look like?

Lincoln said, "The best way to destroy an enemy is to make him a friend, and the best way to make someone a friend is to give them that accolade in your mind." Here is a clue. You give the Monster a BOB (Benefit of the Benefit). Figure it is doing its best and its intention is to be helpful. It just hasn't yet graduated from charm school.

You could wonder, *What is this well-meaning but unskilled aspect of me? How can I process the crude message through my wisdom and make good use of it?*

Remember me waking up in the middle of the night because the sky was falling? The anxiety got me up and got me going to my checkbook. Asleep I was not engaged in doing, so the Worry Monster had an easier time of getting my attention. Maybe it was not the Monster, but me who needed a 2x4 upside the head. Maybe it's all okay.

Perhaps you can play with your inner parts. You can choose to have a conversation with Fear.

You: Hello Fear ... what are you trying to tell me?

Fear: Pay attention ... this is new to us.

You: Do I need more info?

Fear: Yes, when in new territory, proceed with caution.

Well, it seems Fear is not such a bad egg. Just doing its protector gig.

Imagine you are Glinda the Good Witch and you have gathered your inner family around the center of Munchkin Land. There they are. All those distorted messages of love and goodness. Awww, nothing to be afraid of at all. Not when you open your heart and welcome them. Perhaps you'll be given a treat from the Lollipop Guild because you are kind.

Or perhaps, when met with kindness, your Monsters will take flight like the Flying Monkeys did when the Wicked Witch of the West melted into nothingness. Released from her tyranny, liberated from the roles they were cast in, they took off free to explore life in new ways.

You won't know until you experiment with loving all aspects of you. Give them a BOB, knowing they are well-meaning. Open up to the gifts hidden behind the belching flames and the scary head projected onto the wall.

Some quotes you might enjoy:

When people shine a light on their monster, we find out how similar most of our monsters are. ... When people let their monsters out. ... it turns out that we've all done or thought the same things, that this is our lot, this is our condition.

~ *Anne Lamott*

I must learn to love the fool in me — the one who feels too much, talks too much, takes too many chances, loves and hates, hurts and gets hurt, promises and breaks promises, laughs and cries.

~ *Theodore Isaac Rubin*

Love is the only force capable of transforming an enemy into a friend. We never get rid of an enemy by meeting hate with hate; we get rid of an enemy by getting rid of enmity. By its very nature, hate destroys and tears down; by its very nature, love creates and builds up.

~ *Martin Luther King*

39. Get It Off Your Chest

*When, after free-form writing, you realize that you have
been carrying excess weight or baggage, rejoice
in the feeling of freedom.*

John-Roger

༉

Sometimes the brain just won't stop! Running around the block 100 times, mowing the neighbor's lawn, cleaning the house, counting your blessings, and still the mind drones on. What's a person to do?

Get it off your chest! I have a way for you that really works, if you work it. It is called free-form writing. I learned it from a book called *Spiritual Warrior* by John-Roger. I have made good use of this tool and have shared it with many clients over the years.

It is a process of dumping out the contents of Crazy Brain and making space for creativity, insight and wisdom. From this space of clearing, peace is present, and clarity as to choices and actions can be revealed.

HERE'S WHAT YOU DO

Do it in private. Lock the doors if you have to. Take your time. Put your phone on airplane mode. Disconnect from anything that might interrupt you. Create a time/space for you to be alone with you. Light a candle. Invite the Magnificent Mystery to be with you and guide the session in service to your greatest good. Set an intention to write yourself *free.*

Set a time. A minimum of 15 minutes is good. Up to an hour gooder.

Sit down with a paper and pen (do not use a pencil, the tip might break — and no computer). Ask for whatever is for your highest good to occur. Turn yourself over to your wisdom.

Set a timer and go. Don't think. Just write. Thoughts come into the mind and you write them down, as if you are writing a letter. You may not get all the letters for the words onto the paper. You may write chr for chair or prbm for problem.

The writing kinesthetically assists in releasing patterns and negativity. You are freeing the stored up crazy thinking from the body.

If you get stuck, write it out. *I wonder what I should write, this is stupid, I am blank right now, why am I doing this, blank, blank, blank, pink bananas, this is beyond stupid now, turkey feathers, Thanksgiving last year I was ... etc.* Keep writing until the thought flow begins again. Write continuously.

As the thoughts come up, they could have strong emotion. The emotions might change. You may go from anger to fear to hurt to laughter. Any and all of it is okay. Keep writing.

You may find yourself writing forcefully. That is okay. That is why you are using a pen. You may not be able to read your handwriting. It doesn't matter. You are not going to read it. You are releasing. Letting go. Moving on.

I have had times when I became so drowsy, I thought I'd fall asleep right there. *Keep going.* My handwriting was illegible. I could hardly keep the pen on the paper. *Keep writing.* I was pulling out yuck that had been deeply buried.

When you get through RIP IT UP and burn it (or second choice, flush it).

Let me be very clear about this. DO NOT READ IT ... BURN IT. You LET THE PAPER GO into the fire. If you cannot burn it, tear it up into a bazillion pieces and FLUSH THE PAPER. You wouldn't look at your sick after you spewed it up, would you? This is akin to letting go of toxins when you have been ill. Bye-bye Crazy Brain residue. FLUSH or BURN.

Let it go.

You can say aloud or to yourself while the paper is burning, or the water is swirling — I forgive myself for judging myself and anyone else. I release my judgments into the flames. I choose peace.

> *NOTE: Sometimes as the stuff clears, inspiration might come through. Great. Set that page aside and rewrite it later in a special place. Throw away or burn the original.*

Don't share what you wrote with anyone else. Don't even think about what came out. *It doesn't matter.* It's gone now. It has gone back to the nothingness from which it came.

Onward.

You may experience tremendous relief. Stand up and stretch. Breathe into the empty spaces. Don't even think about what had been there. Who cares? It is gone now. Just let it go.

Move on with your life. You are done with that. Complete.

Take a walk. Do a happy dance. Go make dinner.

* If you decide to take this on, something I encourage you to do, please go here for more in-depth info: www.msia.org/experience/free-form-writing

40. Give Up

Attend to that which you can impact directly with change,
wisdom and good outcomes. The rest, do not take
it on. Leave it. Leave it to God.

America Martinez

ॐ

Give it up. Sacrifice the disturbance. Often that is all that is required. Move on. Shift your focus. Look someplace else. Listen to the silence. Give it up to the Magnificent Mystery. Let it go.

There is a saying, "Let go and let God." What does that mean? It means relax and be patient. It means allowing the Magnificent Mystery the space to create miracles in Its own timing, not in yours. It means trusting that life is *for* you. If you relax and open, you will be available to receive the blessings. It means quieting the mind so you can recognize something even greater than you can imagine.

There was a time when I was in a relationship that had not yet resolved itself, yet I knew it was over. It was a complicated circumstance. I knew it would take a while to unravel. I asked my mentor how to deal with it and he told me, "Take a bath and have a beer." What did he mean? Smiling, I realized he was telling me that the conditions would in fact resolve and I could choose to relax and be patient.

Not always an easy task. Impatience can be seen as a *disease* in that it puts us out of ease. Life does itself on its own terms, not much caring about our demands or expectations. Learning how to trust the flow of life takes practice.

It takes more than practice and discipline to change the filtering mechanism in the brain, trusting there is goodness in every experience. It also takes courage. It is courageous to trust the unknown, to give up believing that everything that doesn't go according to plan is a problem rather than a blessing. It takes wisdom to open into the possibility that something greater is on the way. We must be willing to seek good, to see good, and leave the rest alone.

Learning to relate to life as a *for me* process, trusting I will make good use of disturbance, brings me to peace and calm. It's easier for me to relax and be patient. I find myself focusing on my blessings and choosing to live in gratitude.

41. Being a Great Fool

If you concentrate on finding whatever is good in every situation, you will discover that your life will suddenly be filled with gratitude, a feeling that nurtures the soul.

Rabbi Harold Kushner

༈

Have you ever been given a gift, wrapped with paper and tied with a ribbon, and *not* opened it? I doubt it. We are eager to see what is inside the pretty package. What if the gift came in a paper bag that was stained with grease spots from french fries that had been sitting in there since yesterday? The giver of the gift recycling the bag to wrap your gift. Might it still be appealing?

What if what was inside each wrapping, the one with the pretty paper and the greasy paper bag, was exactly the same? Once you opened the gift, would you value it any less? In either case you will throw away the wrapping and keep what is inside. The gift is not the wrapping.

Let's look at gratitude and how it is the great transformer. The choice to be grateful can shift our experience of despair to the awareness of the blessings of the moment. It can move us from a sense of lack to that of abundance. From sadness to delight. Gratitude is a marvel. Envision a magic wand with power to transform your experience in an instant.

One day I was pondering this tool. I heard the word *grateful* in my head and it sounded like Great Fool. That made me laugh. Indeed, I can be considered a Great Fool when I choose gratitude for my challenges, and for my so-called hardships.

We usually say thank you for the gift *before* we unwrap the present. What if we expanded this ritual? What might happen if we express gratitude for whatever we receive? Especially that which we have been complaining about. By leading with gratitude, we are beginning to unwrap the gift.

I do this. An example: a winter when it was colder here in Chicago during the day than it was in Siberia at night. The weather folks nicknamed us "Chiberia." People everywhere were complaining. I, on the other hand, found the experience fascinating. It seems I was a Great Fool.

Thank you, Mother Nature, for this frigid weather. When I led with gratitude, I began to notice how beautiful the snow was. It vividly sparkled in the sun because of the bitterly cold temperatures. I appreciated the stillness of the moment, the quiet of the earth. I realized, though, everything above the surface seemed empty and vast. The frozen earth was doing its job of gestating the spring, getting ready for the next growing season, preparing for springtime awakening.

I saw how this all was a reflection of my own experience at that time. The outer was chilled, slow moving and awkward. Yet inside there was new life waiting to be birthed when the timing was right. I began, Great Fool that I am, to enjoy each day of winter, amazed at yet another day of record cold weather. Noticing how I was enduring, I claimed endurance as an inner strength. I saw my tenacity, resilience, and resolve and grew to appreciate these gifts in me. I witnessed my resourcefulness as I created ways to get things done, inviting support from unexpected places. It became a version of an out-door adventure training, though I was spending most of my time indoors.

Everywhere I went, folks were complaining about what was — the frigid cold. I wondered if the griping about it would change the temperature. I became aware of how much of my life I had spent arguing with reality, that which was out of my control, rather than finding a way to enjoy the moment, or choosing to take action (like moving to Southern California). I was grateful to notice that this time I was doing something different.

That winter turned into a great blessing. It hit me hard at first and then something happened. I chose gratitude. Then I worked to shed the wrapping so I could enjoy what had been given.

What about you? What is a hardship you are experiencing? Are you willing to find something to be grateful for?

Better yet, start with gratitude. Begin with *thank you for this experience* and discover where it takes you.

ॐ ℘ ℘ ॐ ॐ ℘

RX: Do This — Become a Great Fool

- Practice gratitude for blessings which haven't as yet been recognized

- Trust Magnificent Mystery has got this, and all is well … even if you cannot see it … yet

- Take off the greasy wrapping paper to receive that which has already been given

- Be a Great Fool

42. GreatFullness

Love wholeheartedly, be surprised, give thanks and praise — then you will discover the fullness of your life.

Brother David Steindl-Rast

ॐ

"I don't have to get something to be grateful" one of the participants in my *"Creating a Thank-You Life"* workshop declared.

She continued, "I can just *be* grateful!"

We all can.

We create a *Thank-You Life* by how we show up in relationship to what is. No matter what is going on Out-There, we can choose to be grateful In-Here. In other words, regardless of adverse circumstances we can live in joy and be at peace.

Being disturbed doesn't make it better. What makes it better is a good attitude, such as the attitude of gratitude and of looking for the good.

How you might wonder, if Out-There is chaotic and not what I want.

Well, let me tell you a story.

NOW A STORY

Years ago, I was working with a doctor. He told me his late wife died of cancer. He shared with me a gift she had given him at the end of her life, that he cherishes to this day. One day he came home and, as was his usual re-entry pattern, he began by telling her all that had not gone the way he had wanted and dropped a load of complaints at her feet.

Lying on the couch resting, her response to him was, "Sweetheart, problems exist in the world of the living."

Those words woke him up.

Problems come with living. Life is a series of situations that challenge us. We have a choice. We can see the situation as on opportunity to creatively engage. We can look for what is possible and use the situation as creative material.

Unless we don't want to. Unless we want to complain about what is and argue with our circumstances. Unless we want to suffer.

We all have done that. Well I have. I've banged my head against the wall demanding a door appear — ow — walking away with a headache and blaming the wall for hurting me.

There is another way. I can recognize the wall is solid and find a different way to get to the other side. Perhaps I will become an inventor of something that hasn't yet been created, because I choose to persevere, take action and use my creativity to find my way through to what is *next*.

No one really knows the future. We can imagine something other than what is and trust we can contribute positively to our lives. (The Romans struggling to walk on muddy roads, paved them.)

Difficulties are not personal. None of us is exempt from experiencing negativity and adversity. What is personal is how we choose to deal with what is occurring. This is where we develop mastery. Mastery in life is not about avoiding adversity or challenges. It is about Calming Down and Lifting Up. Learning life skills, so that you are resilient, responsive and resourceful when life does what it does.

Overcoming challenges and designing new ways of being can help us grow. We can let our attempt to make it past the immovable wall, be a moment to pause, take a breath and wonder:

- How is this serving me?

- What choices are available to me now?

- How can I design myself and my actions anew?

We could choose to be grateful for that which calls us into creativity and wonder, *Hmmm, what now? What is possible? What is my next action?*

Focusing on *up* leads to gratitude for falling *down*. Standing back up shows me what I'm made of: that which is enduring, strong, courageous, tenacious, and keeps getting back up one more time. It is worth falling down to discover what is true and real.

Problems can become possibilities that lead to projects and next actions. This equals a plan for Living by Design. Choose to welcome problems as situations to engage creatively with a consequence of having a body and living another day. You can be grateful just because.

You can be grateful you have circumstances. You are here and here is alive. Alive is engaged and engaged invites creativity. Creativity is fun and …

Thank you, problems, I see you as gifts. Gifts to inspire creativity, turning stumbling blocks into steppingstones.

Here's to claiming your *Thank-You Life*!

43. Problems are Good for You

You are here to solve problems from a
loving consciousness.

John-Roger

ॐ

The above quote landed in my inbox and I wondered, can life be that simple? In hindsight, I can see my life has been a series of problems that I, based on results, have overcome.

A younger version of me was not skilled at managing problem solving. I would avoid engagement. Like a small child putting her hands over her eyes, if I couldn't see it, it doesn't exist. I found out that strategy didn't work. The problems were still there, only more challenging.

I would get anxious when I faced a circumstance that was unfamiliar. I would freak, eek! The sky is falling and I don't know how to catch it. I don't know what to do.

Crazy Brain on steroids.

NOW A STORY

I used to have a 116-mile round trip drive to my Chicago office. At the end of my drive I landed in a cozy home, nestled in rolling hills, overlooking an ancient farmhouse with a pasture full of wildflowers in the spring and summer.

You can see the drive was worth it. Coming home was a joy.

I kept myself engaged while driving by listening to lectures and books. Great fun. I often didn't know where the time had gone.

I was listening to Pat Allen talking about our brain neurology. Dr. Allen is a psychologist, yet this story is about her mother-in-law who had begun to lose her eyesight. The less she was able to see, the more her mental function diminished. She could no longer do the daily crossword puzzle or read.

Pat's solution was to get her a dog and a never-ending supply of audio books. In a short while the woman's mental faculties gradually returned.

Dendrites are at the very end of our brain neurons. These dendrites will wither if not used in three days.

It's the ol' "use it or lose it" phenomenon. The good news is that a dendrite also will *grow* in three days.

That's what happened to Pat's mother-in-law. She began to stimulate her brain again by having to solve problems. Pat had given her a problem. A dog to care for.

The effects of the dog, plus the audiobooks, led to the woman growing dendrites like crazy.

After listening to this story, I was confronted by a 'problem.' I noticed my initial response was to feel frustrated, as I was stopped in my moving forward. *Oy, a problem to solve — and I was planning on doing something else.* That sorta thing.

But what happened next was interesting. I shifted to seeing the problem as an opportunity to grow more dendrites!

And then I started to laugh. Maybe I might grow enough dendrites to remember where I put my blue scarf which I am still looking for, or why I came into this room, or to turn the stove off, or ...

Over time I learned to meet my circumstances with curiosity. I learned problem solving is fun. It calls upon my creativity. I love figuring things out. I learned that I could pretty much figure out anything. Including who to ask for help when assistance was needed.

It was when I believed I should know before I had the experience, that got me in trouble. When I accept that I don't know, I relax. When I relax, I find my mind is open. When my mind is open, I am available to receive inspiration. This shift helps me see possibilities in problems. Once I have the vision of what is possible, I can create a project and design actions that will lead me to that outcome.

What about you? Do you think you need to know what you don't know before you learn how to know it?

No one knows before we know. The expectation that we should know makes us anxious, inept and unimaginative. Not a resourceful state at all.

Meeting the unknown with creativity and wonder is a resourceful state. We engage with action and produce a result. Circumstances change because of our engagement. We look at the outcome and decide if there is more action to take. This is how we Live by Design. Choosing and acting in relationship to the situation we are in.

We see possibility in problems. We turn our vision of possibility into a project. Taking continuous action towards our vision leads us to creating what we want.

Or something even better.

44. Crunchy

*I would maintain that thanks are the highest
form of thought, and that gratitude is happiness
doubled by wonder.*

G.K. Chesterton

☙❧

Life *is* upsetting and that is a *good* thing. How else can we grow and expand? When the snake is shedding its skin, I imagine it feels restricted as it pushes against the familiar and grows into something new. Something *next.* Growing is an unfolding, an expansion. Growth occurs through disturbance and discomfort.

A client was telling me *this is hard,* referring to the growth occurring in an intimate relationship. Not only was this a new relationship, she was choosing to show up differently than she had in the past. She was learning to be true to herself while sharing with another. This was a big classroom for her.

"Why is it hard? What does that mean?" I asked.

She realized it only meant it was new, different, unfamiliar.

"Why call that hard? Why isn't that fun? Exciting? Even joyous?"

"Hmmm," was her response.

We define our experience by the words we use, by how we language our world. Language creates our reality. Use different words and we create a different experience. Perhaps instead of hard, my client could see her process as exciting.

Back to anxietment. Eek Oh Boy!

I told her "Life is crunchy."

Imagine stepping in a puddle that has become ice. It crunches under your weight, breaking up into pieces, allowing it to thaw more quickly. What if *crunchy* was seen as what happens when we melt open and flow into *next?* This is how we are designed. Only hard if we say so — or not hard at all.

The Comfort Zone Monster calls it hard with a whiny voice, *It's haaaarddddd!!! Whaaa!* This part doesn't want crunchy. It doesn't want flow or expansion. It wants life to stay the same while complaining about what is wrong with current circumstances. Talk about Crazy Brain.

I call this the Zone of the Groan. Crazy Brain chasing its tail going nowhere, a.k.a. the Hamster Wheel of Hades. Thought driven disturbance pretending it is doing, and not doing anything but adding upset to upset.

Growing up into *next* is about embracing the crunchy, *including* the part that thinks this is hard. Learn to enjoy the crunchy. It is my favorite kind of nut butter and it is delicious. Those nuggets of goodness bursting open with surprise flavor ... What if you choose to experience your life that way?

Crunchy, breaking open, growing into *next*. Not comfortable at all, and so what? Skiing down Taos mountain in 20-degree weather, packed inside layers of clothes with boots strapped into polished wood, navigating giant bumps called moguls — this does not sound comfortable at all, yet I call it exhilarating.

I'm still learning to ski the mountain of my life. At times, I forget and attempt to hold on to what was. Eventually I realize I'm holding onto nothing. Life has moved on to what is now. Letting go into *here and now,* I surrender to the moment. Often, if not always, I discover life to be better than I had imagined. But only if I'm willing to look for the blessings that are *here and now.* Willingness is key.

It is the willingness to discover what is here for you; choosing to look for the gifts in the now. Like children on Easter Sunday with baskets in hand, they go out looking for eggs, knowing that if they look, they will find them. Finding eggs is fun for the little ones, not hard. No matter what the experience is — even if they are bundled up with a winter coat on top of their Easter best — they are on an adventure of discovery

What about you?

Are you willing to find the gifts in the crunchy as you shed your skin while growing into *next?* Are you willing to look for what is waiting for you to discover? Is it really hard to be moved by life into your next best self?

Maybe, or maybe not at all.

ର ℘ ℘ ଧ ର ℘

RX: Do This — Own Your Upset

- When you notice you are upset, say to yourself, *I am upsetting myself.* Now look and see how you are doing that. It could sound like,

I'm scaring myself, or *I'm making myself angry.* Own the fact that you are doing it. If you are doing it, you can also do something else.

- Sing a silly song about how you are upsetting yourself while you do a polka around the room.

- Once you calm down, you can write a note of gratitude to That Which Breathes You. Thank you for the blessings of my well-being *here and now.* Feel free to include blessings you would like to experience, including the statement, *This, or something equal to, or greater, for the highest good of all concerned.*

- Optional: You may want to journal what you discover.

45. Just the Next Step

The trees do not strive to bloom and yet they always do.
What if you allowed your next to come?

Allison Crowe

൧ൕഌ

I become tranquil when I realize all I need to do is take the next step. What might that step be, I wonder? When I go a bit slower, practice patience, and take time to wonder, the next action usually appears. Just the next step.

In our world there are sometimes too many choices. Often, we can freeze and not take action. Just do the best you can. Good enough is fine. Make a decision, the best you can. Decide. It will quiet you. If the decision works out, great. If not, you get to choose again. The brain will quiet when you direct it with your decision making. Next, next, next. Staying in action. One step at a time.

I'm reminded of the story of Hansel and Gretel. If you haven't been a little kid in a while let me remind you of the tale.

Hansel and Gretel are the young children of a poor woodcutter. When a great famine settles over the land, the woodcutter's second wife decides to take the children into the woods and leave them there to fend for themselves because the kids eat too much. The woodcutter opposes the plan but finally, and reluctantly, submits. They are unaware that in the children's bedroom, Hansel and Gretel have overheard them. After the parents have gone to bed, Hansel sneaks out of the house and gathers as many white pebbles as he can, then returns to his room, reassuring Gretel that all will be well.

The next day, the family walk deep into the woods. While walking Hansel lays a trail of white pebbles. After their parents leave them, the children wait for the moon to rise and then follow the pebbles back home.

The story goes on. The Grimm brothers don't disappoint, including, as is their trademark, a bit of gore, implied cannibalism and horrid death. The part of the story I want to emphasize is the simple act of following the stones, one stone at a time, leading the children out of the dark forest and into the light, returning home.

There's no need to focus on the past in order to create a better future. Instead, look to the future. Who would you like to become? What would you like to experience? Now create new actions, change your behavior, make new choices in the now.

The truth is you can't foresee your future. If you look in hindsight and compare it to right now, my guess is your current reality is better than you could have imagined. I trust you have come further and created more blessings in your life than you may have envisioned. This is also true moving forward.

Follow the white pebbles. Take the next step.

ॺ ॾ ॼ ॿ ॽ ॾ

RX: Do This — Nexting, Just the Next

Let's wonder together.

- What if there are white pebbles already laid down for you by a part of you that already knows where you are going?

- What if your job is to find the next stone and *allow* yourself to be led out of the darkness and into the light?

- What if you see the white pebbles as clues in a treasure hunt? Your job is to find just the next pebble. Once found, the next clue will reveal itself. Might you take on a mood of wonder and play? Might you play on the way to *next,* fully engaged in the discovery right now?

- How might your life change if you choose to engage in *Nexting,* just the next step?

- And then the next.

- And then the next ...

46. Empty Next

*There is a beautiful tension in all creation between
letting go and forming, the pushing and pulling of
color and sound and everything imaginable.*

Janet Morgan

ༀྀ

A client is about to release her child into the world for the beginning of his journey into adulthood. Concurrently, she is launching herself into the rest of her life as she, too, will be venturing into the next phase with an empty nest.

I was about to email her and before I pushed send, I reread the message to make sure I hadn't made any typos, or that my auto-correct helper (which isn't always helpful) didn't do some mischief to my words. While scanning the document I saw the words *'empty next'* instead of 'empty nest.'

Hmmm ... that gets my attention.

Empty next.

I was called to wonder and turn my attention inwardly to see what is revealed.

Empty next ... hmmm.

Out of the quiet within, an awareness appears. I saw *empty next* as another way to describe Participatory Surrender. Surrender, to me, is part of the creative process.

Have I confused you? Do you think surrender is a hands above your head giving up? Lots of folks hold that thought. I used to, which is why I resisted the process of surrender for so long. I thought it meant I was saying *yes* to victimhood (another example of *just because I think it, doesn't mean it is true*).

I've come to learn the opposite is true. Participatory Surrender involves having a vision, taking a step towards that intention, and then giving up to that which is greater. This opens up a willingness for something even better to appear than I might be able to imagine. Taking action without expectations or demands. Allowing space for the next white pebble to appear.

To me I am giving up to my *co-creator* the essential Creative Energy that breathes me, trusting that only that which will serve my highest good will occur. I take an action in a direction I want to go, holding in my heart that this or something equal to, or greater, for the highest good will occur. I empty myself to receive.

Empty nexting allows me to relax and open as I move through my life. A greater sense of ease and possibility appears. There is more space just by taking action and letting go, giving up and paying attention for *next* to appear.

TIME TO PAUSE

Turn your attention within.

Notice your breathing.

Observe what is present.

Take a conscious breath into your belly.

Exhale.

Remind yourself: *You are not your Crazy Brain.*

You are Something Greater.

Continue.

47. Choosing Joy

When CHEESE gets its picture taken, what does it say?

George Carlin

ॐ

Joy is always present. Joy isn't the absence of disturbance, it is the awareness of the presence of my own true heart, my essence, the Magnificent Mystery, regardless of circumstances.

Circumstances constantly change. The only thing in life that is constant is change. Yet there is a changeless state that is always present, that which doesn't come and doesn't go. It is a resource to each of us.

Changing circumstances are similar to ocean surface, constantly moving. If we pay attention to life only at the surface of experience, we find ourselves bouncing around like a buoy floating on a choppy ocean. Instead, the anchor of the buoy is deeply rooted into the bottom of the ocean — in stillness.

In any moment you could drop your awareness and attend to the stillness at the depth of you. You could do it now.

Let me show you how. Look at your left hand. Just take a moment and move your eyes from these words and bring your attention to your left hand for a few seconds.

Now take the attention you gave to your left hand earlier and direct it to the still place inside of you. Some find closing their eyes helpful. Give yourself time to locate the stillness, the calm, the quiet within.

What do you discover?

For me, I find a space that is expansive, clear and free. I also meet the joy that is, just because I am. It isn't something learned. It isn't something created. It is something I turn my attention to and allow into my awareness. Joy is always present. It is the truth of who we are, for our essential energy is joy.

Can you feel it? If not, pay attention until you do. It's a gift you give to yourself that has value beyond measure.

Joy is one of the most powerful healers on the planet and it is generated from within; no prescription necessary. Joy heals and restores. It regenerates and nourishes. Joy helps our whole being smile.

NOW A STORY

Have you ever seen a movie where a person was hurriedly walking down the street in the rain, under an umbrella or holding a newspaper over their head as if it were going to keep them dry? Suddenly, a car speeds down the street, careens into a puddle and POW, that person is now a soaking mess.

Well, that person was me, as a silver pick-up truck plowed through a puddle at a bazillion miles an hour oblivious to little ol' me doing my best to stay tucked under my umbrella. My whole left side was soaked and in an instant the wet turned cold.

I noticed there was a part of me that wanted to get upset. It was a thought wanting to go on a rant about that so-and-so. I didn't follow that thought into misery. Instead, I came present in the moment and what I experienced was calm amusement.

Truly.

It was funny.

It was funny to be suddenly on a movie set.

I'm sure there was a hidden camera someplace!

One of my mentors loves to say, if it is going to be funny later, you may as well laugh now. I wasn't thinking of those words so I could make myself laugh (pithy statements are lovely, but they are not really transformative). It is the daily doing, the ongoing shifting into joy, that paves a path to amusement when soaked on the side of the road.

Giggling my way to my car, I mentally changed my plans due to my new soggy circumstances. I decided to go home, take a hot shower, and tuck in on my comfy couch nestled into the warmth of my wood-burning fireplace. So, what if it was the end of May? I was chilled and the idea of warming up and cozying-in made me happy.

What are you upset with now that in a day or two, or maybe longer, when you look back on your upset, you will see as funny? Why wait until then? Have yourself a giggle now. Getting upset about it isn't going to make it any easier to deal with, whatever it is. But joy — happy — that's a whole other realm. That is where the creative mind opens and offers solutions to our troubles.

So, when upset, do a happy dance; invite yourself to be amused. Or invite a Muse (a creative influence) to come play with you. Ask her to bring a blessing of inspiration.

Truly, I was inspired to cozy up to my fire. It was a lovely evening. Thank you, reckless man driving that truck. Thank you, Muse, for writing this story. Thank you, reader, for considering that you too can giggle your way out of soggy circumstances.

ꝺ ꝼ ꝭ ꝫ ꝭ ꝼ

RX: Do This — Choose Joy

Joy isn't the absence of disturbance. Joy is the presence of who you truly are. Learn to shift your attention from the choppy waves of your outer circumstances and drop to the inner depths of calm and peace.

At the end of the day, capture, by writing down, moments of joy you experienced during that day.

Remember: what we focus on grows. Writing down moments of joy will program your brain to notice more joy, which will lead to even more joy, which will lead you to living in joy regardless of circumstances!

48. Stand Up

*Life shrinks or expands in proportion
to one's courage.*

Anais Nin

༖

Take a moment to reflect on your life. Regardless of your time on this planet, you are still here. No matter what has befallen you, however many ways you have stumbled or been knocked down, you have stood up again. Every single time.

The evidence? You are still here. Therefore, you can count on yourself to stand back up as many times as you fall. The fact that you have always been able to regroup and rebound from adversity can give you the confidence and assurance that you will continue to stand back up again and again.

It takes courage. Our friend Dorothy demonstrated courage. That doesn't mean she wasn't shaking in her ruby slippers now and again. It *does* mean she persevered in spite of having the shakes, because if she didn't keep going, she would never get home to Kansas. Kansas is what her heart desired more than anything else.

Courage is an action of the heart. I see courage as the willingness to endure in the face of adversity, determination to achieve a goal in spite of seeming obstacles. It takes courage to risk, invest in, be in action, participate, do what it takes, take action on your desire, get up one more time than you fall, keep going even when there are Mind Monsters screaming and monkeys flying around your head laughing at you, complaining, griping, whining and moaning. What do they know? They haven't been right yet. You are still here. The sky still is in the sky.

Sure, your life didn't turn out the way you thought it would. Ask anyone. Neither has theirs. So what? *Now what?* Keep going. Challenge yourself to see how your life *did* turn out perhaps even *greater* than you could ever have imagined.

Your thinking isn't real. Reality is more generous than is your mind. If you can't find the goodness that is here, keep looking. The blessings of your life, as it is, are waiting to be discovered. Perhaps you are looking in the wrong direction.

49. We're All On Our Way to Dead

What a wonderful life I've had.
I only wish I'd realized it sooner.

Colette

ℛℬ

I have lots of clients disturbed about something or other. It could be their boss, their spouse, one of their troublesome kids. Perhaps their pants are too tight, or they are struggling with a colleague at work. For some people it's the news. For *lots* of people it's the news.

I was talking to a client who was very disturbed by a recent bulletin. She had read an article claiming there was a purposeful scheme to diminish the population of the planet in a big way.

Wow, that's an interesting point of view! Just because the story is in print or on the internet doesn't mean it's true. Just because these words are in a book on paper, or in an electronic document, doesn't make them truth. Checking it out and finding out what works for you is what makes things real. It's your job, and mine, to discover what is useful.

Rather than reporting factual information, the news often is not much more than other people's thinking. Other people's thinking being broadcast in an attempt to get the reader to think the same thoughts.

Something like the population of the world coming to an end in a big and sudden way is quite the story. I wondered aloud how anybody knew these things. Apparently, someone is really invested in their thinking and has decided to share their thinking as if it is truth. The mind is a meaning making machine and loves its opinions. Another example of humanity investing in thinking, forgetting our thoughts are not reality. That is a fundamental mistake. I trust that by now, in reading this book, you have become more aware that what we think may not be true at all.

No one wants to suffer. We would never hurt ourselves on purpose. We are all doing the best we know how to do. We have been taught to believe our thoughts. It's innocent, well-meaning, and an error in approach.

It is our thinking that is in the way of accessing the source of well-being, wisdom and goodness in our lives. I taught my client about giving herself some space between her sense of reality and somebody else's thinking. I suggested she consider that she doesn't want to absorb other people's points of view, especially if it's disturbing. I don't like hot, as in spicy, food. I don't eat it; it upsets my belly. I also don't watch gory horror movies because I have nightmares. Perhaps my client would choose not to ingest other people's opinions that upset her. Read the news, if that is what she wants, just be careful not to eat at the table of doom.

The reality is we are all on our way to dead whether there is some nasty scheme out to get 7+ billion of us in one fell swoop, or something else is going to cause our bodies to stop breathing. No matter how, I'm on my way to dead. So are you. What are we going to do about it?

Life goes on: when we rest, when we are joyful, when we are sad, arguing with what is, or allowing life to unfold on life's terms. No matter what the news of the day is, life continues. Snow falls, the ground freezes, we cozy up indoors and then spring blossoms open, and so do we. And with all that coming and going, we are on our way to dead.

Imagine driving on a dark road without a light on. All sorts of shadows and movements could create a disturbance in the mind that makes things up. We take dominion over our circumstances by shining light into our lives, the light of our peaceful presence, the light of our loving, the light of our gratitude.

Life is like driving from here to there. It is a great distance and we can't see the end. We don't have to. All we need to do is keep throwing light in front of us and follow the headlights. Eventually we will get there.

I'd like to take my last breath with a big smile on my face. Perhaps go out on a big HaHa. Something catches my tickle bone and I'm uproariously laughing and next thing I know, oh my goodness, I'm dead. That was fun.

No matter how you are going to breathe your last breath, how do you want to spend your life between now and then? Do you want to be fretting about somebody else's opinions, perhaps about the world coming to an end? Or would you like to be a joyful participant in the precious gift of life you have?

The past does not have to equal the future. Once we know better, we can do better. You can choose to explore with curiosity and find out for yourself if there is a place of well-being present to you *here and now.* You can choose to pay your attention to that place in you and in others, that feels good, that *is* good.

This could be your last breath.

I don't know.

Neither do you.

So, what are you going to do about it?

50. Service: The Fastest Way Up

If you want to lift yourself up, lift up someone else.

Booker T. Washington

ᘉᑭ

Little things can make a big difference in our life and the lives of others. Let yourself wonder what you might do for another person. A smile, getting them a cup of coffee, pulling out a chair, shoveling a walk. The choices are limited only by your imagination. Making a positive difference in the lives of others lifts us up. When we do good, we feel good.

NOW A STORY

As I left my Chicago office, my windshield wipers worked hard clearing large flakes of snow mixed with salt from the roads. Driving home, I saw snow piled up along the roadsides, freshly plowed. Ten miles from my home the snow stopped. As I rounded the corner, I saw my driveway smooth with virgin snow. Pristine, brilliant white. Beautiful to behold and calling me to play. Alas, it was 10:45 at night. While tucking in at some point that evening was a priority, there was no way I could have parked in the garage until the drive was cleared.

Though it was 12 degrees out, my coat was warm, my hat was snug, my mittens toasty. I was happy. My manuscript had been sent for a final edit. My day was filled with wonderful clients. I was full of energy. I was looking forward to burning some fuel by shoveling.

I was clearing the entry to the front door when out of the darkness a man with a shovel appeared. My hackles went up as I wondered who was approaching. It was late. Most folks were asleep.

Tentatively I called out, "Hello?" to which a friendly voice said, "Hi, it's me."

"Oh, hi." I replied, recognizing my neighbor Jim's voice and that I had yet again frightened myself over nothing.

Jim, who had been tucked into his cozy house, had seen me working, put his warm clothes on and grabbed his shovel to join me. Why? To help me out. To be kind.

We had a lovely chat while shoveling, and in no time the drive was clear. We paused to enjoy the almost full moon reflecting gentle winter light onto a few scattered clouds.

I shared my gratitude, and he returned to his home as I went into mine.

Jim's kindness reminded me of a Dalai Lama quote which inspires me, "Be kind whenever possible. It is always possible."

Kindness — it is always possible.

Studies have shown that we are instinctively compassionate. Our brains are wired with an urge to help each other. Human survival has been dependent on our kindness and in learning to cooperate.

Service is any action where we do something for another without expectation of anything in return. In doing so we connect to our joy and nourish our well-being. Serving, for the purpose of giving from the heart, lifts us up to our better selves.

Feeling low, anxious, depressed? Crazy Brain on a rampage? Get out of your own way and focus on someone else. Choose to be kind. Challenge yourself to serve when you are lost in your own thinking. It could be as simple as making a cup of tea for someone, sending a kindhearted text, or extending a smile of welcome.

ANOTHER STORY

I have a client who is a delight. She brings to our conversation wisdom developed from living on this planet more than seven decades. She was sharing how she had to take the bus downtown in order to get blood work prior to an upcoming surgical procedure. It was a long commute with walking to the bus stop, waiting for the bus and traveling twenty-five minutes to her destination. Just as she arrived home after the long journey the phone rang. It was the lab. The technician made an error and the draw was incomplete. They wanted her to return so they could finish.

My client told me she was a little grumpy at first. She didn't want to leave her cozy home where she was just settling in and get back on the bus. She knew she was going to have to go as the surgery was pending, so she decided she was going to choose patience and kindness. She put her coat back on and walked out her front door back to the bus stop.

I asked her to stop her story and tell me how she did that. It is a skill to choose patience in the middle of disturbance.

She said it was tough for her to do, yet she realized she would rather be on the bus enjoying the sun coming in the window than be grumpy. Rather than be unkind when she met the lab technician, her preference was to be pleasant.

I asked her to explain slowly to me how she made that shift.

What I discovered is she decided to give him a BOB (Benefit of the Benefit see chapter 23.) She put herself in his shoes. She imagined him new on the job, messing up, causing her to come all the way back on the bus. She empathized with how bad he must feel.

She knew the young man didn't do it on purpose. He had been gentle with her while drawing her blood. Something she appreciated. She didn't want to make him feel worse than she imagined he was already feeling.

Wow, she made serving him more important than the righteous indignation she initially felt. She was going to have to return to the lab regardless of her attitude. She knew she could return with *againstness* towards this man and the world would agree she'd been done wrong. Instead she lifted up into a place of loving kindness and compassion for the young technician.

We can see her choice provided love and kindness to herself as well. She was the one who got to live in the experience of her attitude. Righteous indignation or loving kindness. Either way she was on the bus headed back for a do-over. In choosing to be kind to him, she served herself as well.

Hmmm, something to notice.

Choosing to walk in another's shoes, experiencing their point of view, allows us the opportunity to expand beyond our own position. From this expanded place we can see there are more options; greater freedom to choose a joyful life.

Back to you (and me). What do we choose? The grumps or kindness? We always have a choice. More than a feeling, kindness is a decision.

What will you choose?

When you forget to go high, that's okay. After all you are human, just like the rest of us. Forgive yourself for forgetting and choose again.

I continue to be amazed at the power of kindness. I have been tracking actions of loving kindness and have discovered service is an antidote to negative thinking. Serving keeps me sane. It gets me out the self-importance fostered by Crazy Brain and into the energy field of Loving.

Service — the fastest way to lift up.

51. Say Yes!

Say yes!

Frankie Bergstein

༈

Play a game with me. Say *yes* to whatever is going on in the moment. See what happens inside of you. Yes, to this traffic. Yes, to looking on the scale and seeing the number is higher than the last check in. Yes, to somebody that's really important not calling back. Yes, to the raccoon raiding the bird feeder, yet again.

Where does YES take you? A friend of mine encourages herself with, *Yay! I get to participate in this. I get to do this.* I love that. Saying yes to life as life is showing up.

Notice what happens in your brain when you say, *I get to do this. I get to be here doing this now.* For me, I notice an immediate upshift into seeing what is here for me and how I can contribute.

Whatever it is you're going through, what would happen if you said YES? Why not find out by experimenting? I encourage you to say YES. Yes, to your husband falling asleep on the couch, again. Yes, to your child coming home with average grades. Yes, to the promotion you just got. Yes, to selling your book to a publisher after 10 years of trying. Yes, to a long relaxing weekend away with just your spouse. Yes, to another day of rain. Yes, Yes, YES!

Perhaps it would Calm you Down and Lift you Up into possibility that is unseen when you're saying no or arguing with what is. Yes, I am willing to see the good *here and now*.

Yes, thank you, yes.

Say yes.

Waking up each morning with a YES!

With a grateful heart saying YES to your life.

Yes, to the creativity that lives within.

Yes, to the joy that is your essence.

Yes, to the beauty that is present now.

Yes, to the possibility of something even greater unfolding throughout this day.

Yes, to discovering the blessings that are *here and now*.

Yes, to the joy that lives in you — that is you.

Yes, to living a good life because who you are at essence is good.

Yes, to the future that welcomes you to step into it each day

Yes, to your willingness to say YES. A willingness to see beauty in yourself, in the day, in your circumstances. Even the difficult, challenging circumstances.

Yes, to discovering the opportunity to grow, develop and expand as a result of participating in your life as it invites the best of you into play.

Yes, to your wisdom, forgiveness, compassion, kindness and loving.

Saying Yes — welcoming this breath — and now this one. What is being revealed to me *here and now?* What is being asked of me? *Here and now.* Listening. Participating. Saying yes. Thank you for this moment I get to say yes to. Living in Joy for the blessings that are.

Yes, yes, yes.

Thank you, thank you, thank you.

52. It is Not in OZ

Instead of searching for what you do not have,
find out instead what it is that you have never lost.

Nisargadatta Maharaj

༚༛

I'm imagining you have seen a headline inviting you to make a purchase that looked something like this:

HOW TO CREATE GREATER ABUNDANCE, SUCCESS, AND PROSPERITY.
CLICK HERE

What do you really imagine you are going to find on the other side of that link? For me, I have found there is nothing there but blah blah blah inviting me to increase the financial abundance, success and prosperity — of the author.

What if we don't have to create any of those things? What if they already exist as the natural state of our beingness? What if all we have to do is take a breath and shift our attention to where those qualities already live inside us? What if you already are abundance?

Out-There is always trying to lure us into leaving Home in order to find something we already have. Facebook, for example, is genius at this. All those posts from Other People doing/having what perhaps we imagine we want. Those cateredto-us ads that are statistically designed to grab our attention while they grab the money.

I do my best to bypass my Facebook homepage on the way to one of the groups I run, and every now and again I'll stumble into the never-ending feed of posts. Sometime later I shake myself out of the stupor I'm in. Then I get back on track to where I was going.

On my way to where I was going. Hmmm, where might that be? Am I really going anywhere? Perhaps I'm already where I want to be. I have just forgotten.

Do you remember what Glinda told Dorothy at the end of the Wizard of Oz?

Dorothy: Oh, will you help me? Can you help me?

Glinda: You don't need to be helped any longer. You've always had the power to go back to Kansas.

Dorothy: I have?

Scarecrow: Then why didn't you tell her before?

Glinda: She wouldn't have believed me. She had to learn it for herself.

Scarecrow: What have you learned, Dorothy?

Dorothy: Well, I — I think that it, that it wasn't enough just to want to see Uncle Henry and Auntie Em — and it's that — if I ever go looking for my heart's desire again, I won't look any further than my own backyard. Because if it isn't there, I never really lost it to begin with! Is that right?

Glinda: That's all it is!

Scarecrow: But that's so easy! I should've thought of it for you.

Tin Man: I should have felt it in my heart.

Glinda: No, she had to find it out for herself. Now those magic slippers will take you Home in two seconds!

Dorothy: Oh! Toto too?

Glinda: Toto too.

Dorothy: Now?

Glinda: Whenever you wish.

Glinda: Then close your eyes and tap your heels together three times. And think to yourself, *'There's no place like Home.'*

The Great and Powerful Oz is not real, and, therefore, cannot take us where we want to go. The journey to something isn't about getting anywhere at all. Out-There is just a distraction from what is already present. Yet the journey down the Yellow Brick Road, in an attempt to discover what we are looking for Out-There, is part of the process of discovering that we have everything we need already In-Here.

There is a Zen teaching about a student who asks the Master: "What can be done about the extremes of weather, the hot and cold?"

The Master replies: "If you are so concerned, why don't you go someplace where there are no variations in temperature?"

I'm writing from the Chicago area where we can have extreme weather in winter. There have been years when we had several days at -20° Fahrenheit without the windchill. I woke up one day to an email from a friend in Oklahoma asking if I was okay. The lead story in the news was that it was colder in Chicago than it was in the Antarctic.

The weather is one of those things that shows us we're not in control of our outer circumstances. Yet we can go to the place where there is no variation in temperature.

Where do you imagine that is?

When you find that place, it can be a life-changing awakening. When you discover the answer, you've come across a priceless treasure, the pearl of great price.

To me, the place where there is no change in temperature is what I'm going to call our true center or essence. This is the calm in the center of all movement, the still point. Some call it Presence. Some call it the Divine, the Soul, the True Self, Home. It doesn't matter what you call It. What matters is you become intimate with that place inside of you.

You've already been there. You may or may not remember. It is beyond thinking, beyond feeling, beyond the movement of the body. It is that which sources our inhale and our exhale. It is the place I have been guiding you to through these many pages.

There's no good, bad, right or wrong in this place. No rules or judgments. No hot or cold, wind or rain, storms or disturbance. It's a place of beingness. Pure awareness.

In this place of true center, it matters not if it's minus 20° Fahrenheit with snow, ice and howling wind. What the news is reporting is irrelevant. Your stubbed toe is unimportant, as is the fact that it is time to have a haircut. This is a place of peace and joy regardless of outer circumstances.

Here is the good news: you've never left.

Just like Dorothy, you imagined yourself in a dream of a faraway land where it is cold and snowing. You forgot where *you* really are.

You, too, never left Home. You are already where you want to be. You don't need to do, be, or have anything, to live in abundance. You don't have to **CLICK HERE.** You are, in this moment, everything you are looking for. If you are not aware of that, perhaps you could shift your focus until you recognize this. All you have to do is turn your attention within, tune into your heart. Take a breath in and call yourself Home.

Sometimes we need help to calm down and learn to embrace the Monsters and discover their gifts. Just like Dorothy made good use of Glinda's guidance as she clicked the ruby slippers and called herself Home, I trust this book has been a Glinda for you.

So — close your eyes — take a breath and remember — you are already Home.

Ahhh ... there is no place like Home.

53. Find the Good

*Look only for the good, for the Divine in people
and things, and all the rest leave to God.*

John-Roger

༂

Now it's time to say goodbye.

Don't just put the book down, use it. Many people told me after reading my last book that they kept it by their bedside to reference when they were stuck. This book is written in a similar way. I designed it so you could open to a chapter and have that chapter be a complete message in and of itself.

Now the work begins. Time to take action and change your life, from the inside out. This isn't just a movie, a YouTube video or a Ted talk. This is your life. Do it. Participate. Show up. Take action. Make mistakes. Take new action. Learn and grow. And use *everything* for your upliftment.

EVERYTHING.

There's no wrong turn because every step gets you to here. Here is present. Come present to the presence that is here. You will find goodness. You will find peace. You will find joy.

Don't attempt to change negativity by being negative about the negativity. That only adds more negativity to what is already occurring. It's not our job to change the negativity in the world. It isn't even our job to change the negativity inside our-selves. Our job is to lift and step into the blessings that already are. In doing so we become a blessing to ourselves and to oth-ers. Just turn your eyes towards that which is good — includ-ing inside yourself.

Seek and ye shall find.

Find the good.

In Conclusion

Baruch Bashan. The blessings already are.

John-Roger

ॐ

One of my favorite hymns contains the words "Let there be peace on Earth and let it begin with me." I want to thank you for stepping forward and saying yes to becoming an everyday, ordinary peacemaker.

The more of us who choose peace, the more peace there will be on Earth.

Perhaps you are now more willing to take time each day and tune into the peaceful presence inside of you. Extend your peace into your life. Don't look for a result or a reward. Just be a peaceful presence, as best you can, throughout your day, throughout your life. Remember, the peace that you are, the peace that you live, the peace that you give — that is the reward. Allow it to flow through you. Recognize it as a gift you give. First to yourself, then extending peace into the world.

May you *be peace* and live in joy.

You are the blessing.

Just for Fun Bonus Story:
Battered Bugs

*Mastery in life is not about avoiding adversity or challenges.
It's about learning life skills, so you are resilient, responsive,
and resourceful when life does what it does. It's about
embracing change while learning, so you can meet
life on life's terms and win.*

From: *Life Happens:*
What are YOU Going to Do About It?

⁂

How the following story came about was clearly orches-trated by the Magnificent Mystery That Breathes Us All.

I was in LAX airport talking to a man as we both waited for our flight at the gate. For whatever reason I was going stand-by. At this point it was clear I wasn't getting out at 5:40pm. Bad weather in Dallas. Over 1,000 flights canceled. The airline doing its best to catch up in the midst of the re-routing mess. I'm number 80 to get on this flight and it doesn't look good. Quite frankly, it is impossible.

The protocol for stand-by is to wait until they don't call you, then get herded over to the next flight. This keeps hap-pening until an open seat is available.

The man I was talking with had been reading a book about battered bugs or something like that. They called the flight and a throng of people gathered to board. The man didn't get up to join the crowd.

We continued to chatter-on about nothing, as happens with strangers. I asked him if he was going stand-by as I was. He said no, he had a boarding pass for the flight. He just didn't want to wait in the jetway.

The throng thinned out and vanished. All had boarded the flight. The man still didn't get up.

A group of three — 2 pilots and one attendant — hurried to the gate. They were quickly escorted onto the plane. At this point, with the scurry of activity, the man decided it was time to board. He casually got up and gathered his belongings. While doing so I said, "I'm sorry about the battered bugs." He hesitated and then connected to what I was saying. He responded, "Oh, this book. Yeah. My friend wrote it. I have to read it. It is terrible."

As he turned to go to the gate I said, "You could read my book. I just finished it." He asked the title while handing his ticket to the gate agent.

I told him, *Life Happens: What are YOU Going to Do About It?*

In that very same moment, the gate agent informed him he didn't make the flight. He had waited too long. There were no seats left on the plane.

Life was happening.

What did he do about it?

He had a tantrum. He threw down his belongings and began yelling at the agents. "I have to get on this flight! I have to get on this flight!"

What do you think? Did he get on the flight?

No. He didn't get on the flight. No amount of screaming and demanding opened the doors to the plane.

It took me a moment to get over the automatic thinking that I was responsible in some way for him having missed the flight. (Oops! Mind Monsters at work.) Once my mind had quieted, I was able to appreciate the irony of the past five minutes. Here he was, life having happened. And yes, he contributed to, if not created, his circumstances, and what was he *doing* about it? Having a fit.

That's not unusual for any of us. None of us is innocent. I know I'm not. When something happens other than what we planned, there *is* an automatic reaction that occurs. The key is *now what?* How are we going to manage the automatic surge of adrenaline that courses through the body? Are we going to have a fit? Are we going to see ourselves as victim to our circumstances? Are we going to hold on to the upset?

There is another choice. Life just happened. In response, *do* something back.

Breathe into peace and calm down. Shift back to quiet where creativity is sourced. Wonder about what now. What can be done *now* that Life has Happened, and circumstances have changed? What is a next action?

I saw this man later at a different gate waiting for the next plane. He was on the phone with someone telling them all about what had happened. He was still upset as he shared his tale of woe — a juicy story about how the airline had done him wrong. Hanging out in *then* instead of being here in *now*.

Ah well. We all get to live in the consequences of our choices. He could have been reading his friend's book. Or maybe mine!

β

Life Happens: What Are YOU Going to Do About It? has won an award and is available at Amazon in paperback and Kindle.

Moving Forward

Congratulations on completing this book. To help you move forward here are some suggestions that may help you lift up:

- Practice peace daily, Calm Down and Lift Up into your greater self by meditating. Set your intention to *be peace* as best as you can throughout the day.

- When upset, own it. Claim the upset as your creation. *Ooo, look, I upset myself.* Observe how you're doing that. Now do something else.

- Do something physical. Walk, run, clean the house, rake leaves, dance, skip, jump. Bake cookies to give away.

- Giving your cookies is an act of service. Give more. Do something for someone else. Send a note of gratitude. Pick up the phone and call. Doing for others gets us out of Crazy Brain. Try it. You'll be amazed.

- Ask for help. You can ask someone who has the skills that can be useful. You can also ask the Magnificent Mystery to lift you into your creative, joyful self.

- Whatever you thought was upsetting you, it probably isn't. So make up something else. Win in your own fantasies.

- Practice breathing into peace throughout the day. Pause, turn your attention to your breath, calm down.

- Even if you're not upset, there is more peace available, and even more than that.

- The peace that you are is the peace that you give. Share your joyful, loving, peaceful presence. Extending the blessing of your calm is a gift. Your presence will facilitate others in calming down and lifting. All you have to do is be.

- Though your presence may assist others in Calming Down and Lifting Up, you can't do it for them. Your presence can be a reminder and support for them to do it for themselves. But only if they want to.

- Allow others the dignity of their choice while you continue to choose peace. You get to live in the consequences of your choices. Choose peace.

- Look for the Easter eggs, the blessings, the gifts. If you look, you will find them.

- Take a big dose of LSD. Laughing, Singing and Dancing.

- Be grateful for the gift of the awareness that you have a choice. You now know you can Calm Down and Lift Up. You have a choice to get off the Hamster Wheel of Hades. Say thank you to *you* every time you make that choice. Be grateful for your willingness to *be peace.*

- Become an Everyday Ordinary Peacemaker. Be peace for the joy of peace. Practice the tools offered in this book. Consider investing in the Calm Down Lift Up course that is rich with resources not found in this book, including short meditations easily incorporated into your life. You can gain access at *www.living-bydesign.com* under *Programs and Events.*

- Write to me at *leslie@living-bydesign.com,* and let me know something you will experiment with from this book. When I receive your email, I will send you a special link for the course that will lower your tuition. My way to say thank you for your willingness to grow in peace.

- Share this book with others. The more of us who choose peace, the more peace there will be in our world. Who do you know who will benefit from having more calm and peace in their lives? How might their peace contribute to yours? Perhaps you would share information about this book on your social media pages. *Thank you.*

Post Script

Please feel free to reach out. Your success is my joy! If you have any questions, email me. I usually respond within 24 hours. If you haven't heard back, **reach out again**. That spam folder can be a bit annoying.

What else? Hmmm ... I told you your success is my joy. Reach out. My email address is *leslie@living-bydesign.com*. Sign up for my newsletters. Stay in touch.

This book is a meal all by itself. You do not have to purchase the *Calm Down Lift Up* course in order to be served by reading, and *if* you want to partake, write to me. Let me know one thing you will experiment with from this book. When I receive your email, I will send you a special link for the program that will lower your tuition. Oh, I already told you that. Well, I mean it.

RX: Do This
Take a Next Action

BREATHE INTO PEACE

I have found the breath to be one of the Big Power Tools we have in transforming our lives. So much so that I teach a breathing practice to my clients, supporting them in resolving issues, enabling greater access to inner resources of strength, creativity, courage, and spiritual intelligence.

This type of BreathWork is powerful in that it rewires the brain, so you have greater access to human resilience, creativity and wisdom, with increased ease in bypassing the survival brain.

I welcome you to consider the experience of BreathWork as a next step. Private BreathWork sessions with me can be facilitated in person, via video conference, or by phone. I have designed an introductory BreathWork program so you can find out how powerful this work can be for you. The details can be found here: *breathworkwithleslie.com*

Whether you take me up on this offer or not, you have been introduced to several breathing practices throughout this book that can be useful to you — if you use them.

LIVING BY DESIGN TIPS

Sign up for my Living by Design Tips, Practical Tools for Everyday Living, an online newsletter delivered to your inbox with your permission. In addition to receiving the Living by Design Tips eZine, you will also receive a gift from me, something to support you in living by design rather than by default. *lesliesann.com/blog*

BRAIN NOOGLES

A noogle is a brain massage intended to awaken your inner wisdom. Pull a card when your mind is smargled, you need a boost, a lift up, another way to see what is.

49 cards with sayings to support you in lifting up into your intelligence and wisdom. Available at my website on the resource page.

LIVING BY DESIGN SCHOOL

The Living by Design School is an educational resource with the intention of supporting you in developing a philosophy of living that you can use to guide you in your life. There are a series of learning programs designed to support you in evolving into *next*. These courses teach essential life skills to help you navigate the challenges we all face in life.

The Living by Design School teaches practical, useful life skills to support your learning, growth and personal evolution, while creating a good life. A life you love.

Thank Yous

৩৫

Blessings to my Crazy Brain which has tortured me to the point of learning to take dominion and lift up into joy.

Gratitude to my clients who have reflected, over the course of more than 30 years, that calming down is the first step in creating a joyful life.

To all the readers of my first book who shared with me how it helped change their lives for the better. They helped me say YES to this project. Not a trivial task at all. Thank you.

Howard Bresnik for his patience in going through the book with me – word – by – word – by – word. Howard you are a mensch.

Robyn Randle for making an invaluable contribution with her talent, brilliance, precision insight and generous loving heart.

Steve Chandler, who challenged me after my first book was published by suggesting I could write an even better book. Perhaps I have.

Robert McCreight, inspiring joy and play through the gift of words.

John Hagelberg, for his insight, wisdom and confidence.

Beneficent Kris Martin who blesses me abundantly with her encouragement, applause and delight.

Rick Kantor my prizing encourager extraordinaire and for his creative contribution.

Christopher Podhola, assisting me in numerous ways, including helping me write more easily from my heart.

Lynda Otte, my steadfast assistant, now dear friend, my rock of support.

About the Cover

༄ཨ

Some photographs have a subject and others portray a
feeling. 'Ocean Grass at Sunrise' is a simple photo that captures
the feeling at daybreak. A feeling of being refreshed with a
new attitude, and new possibilities.

~ Daniel deMoulin

As I faced the task of visually capturing the contents, I began engaging with resources, playing with possibilities. This required slowing down and allowing the process to unfold, giving space for something greater than I was imagining.

I was introduced to Daniel by way of a photograph he had sent to a dear friend of mine. I was touched with the beauty in the original photo, the aliveness, the joy of awakening, the pervasive peace.

Daniel and I collaborated, and together with the Magnificent Mystery, and Daniel's enormous talent, a cover emerged that holds the joy, peace and creative possibility that is available to us in every moment.

About Leslie Sann

(that's me)

❧

My life is dedicated to guiding people in adopting a practical spiritual approach to living while creating a life they love. For more than 30 years my career has been rich with helping people transform their lives; neutralizing the misery-making-mechanism of their minds into a tool that fosters joy and well-being.

You can call me a brain-pain-exterminator. Imagine a splinter in the mind, a thought that's irritating. This thought is filtering reality in ways that are disturbing. I help extract the disturbing thought. The mind then becomes a useful sorting device. Instead of a misery maker, it becomes a blessing seeker, a joy finder.

Your success *is* my joy. It's how I'm wired. When you go up, I go up. I am gratified seeing other people win and be happy. It's nourishing food for me.

If I can be of service to you please get in touch. Reach out. Tell me what you are creating, maybe where you're stuck. Ask me a question.

May you recognize the blessings that already are,

Leslie

P.S. When you email, I will send you a gift. Just let me know you have read this book, so I can make what I send to you relevant. *leslie@living-bydesign.com*